ELIZABETH MACLEOD
FRIEDA WISHINSKY

COLOSSAL
CANADA

Scholastic Canada Ltd.
604 King Street West, Toronto, Ontario M5V 1E1, Canada

Scholastic Inc.
557 Broadway, New York, NY 10012, USA

Scholastic Australia Pty Limited
PO Box 579, Gosford, NSW 2250, Australia

Scholastic New Zealand Limited
Private Bag 94407, Botany, Manukau 2163, New Zealand

Scholastic Children's Books
Euston House, 24 Eversholt Street, London NW1 1DB, UK

www.scholastic.ca

Library and Archives Canada Cataloguing in Publication
MacLeod, Elizabeth, author
Colossal Canada : 100 epic facts and feats / Elizabeth MacLeod
and Frieda Wishinsky.
ISBN 978-1-4431-2820-9 (pbk.)
1. Canada--Miscellanea--Juvenile literature. I. Wishinsky,
Frieda, author II. Title.
FC58.M32 2015   j971.002   C2014-905335-5

6 5 4 3 2 1   Printed in China 38   15 16 17 18 19

ELIZABETH MACLEOD
FRIEDA WISHINSKY

COLOSSAL CANADA

100 EPIC FACTS AND FEATS

Scholastic Canada Ltd.

Toronto New York London Auckland Sydney
Mexico City New Delhi Hong Kong Buenos Aires

CONTENTS

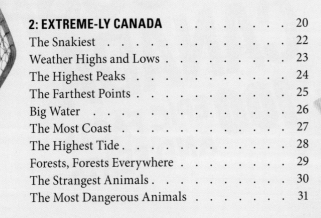

INTRODUCTION

There's no doubt about it. Canada *is* colossal. Not just because it's the second-largest country in the world. Not just because it extends from the Atlantic to the Pacific and up to the Arctic. Not just because it has a varied and magnificent landscape of soaring mountains, mighty rivers, four of the five Great Lakes and vast prairies framed by a big sky. Not just because of its extreme weather, strange creatures, fabulous festivals and innovative inventions.

Most of all, what makes a country colossal is its people. So many Canadians have enriched this country with their skills, ideas, energy, creativity, food, determination, humour and stories. They've made lasting contributions to the world and helped make Canada a country rooted in a fascinating, dramatic past, and ready to face an exciting future.

And that is *truly* colossal!

What makes a country unique? Its rich, fascinating, surprising history. Its food, products, landscape, weather, sports. Most of all, its people. Canada is one of the most diverse countries in the world in land, population and climate. Read on to find out about things that make up what it means to be Canadian, and what makes this vast, varied country so special.

CHAPTER 1

UNIQUELY CANADIAN

What's So Canadian About That?

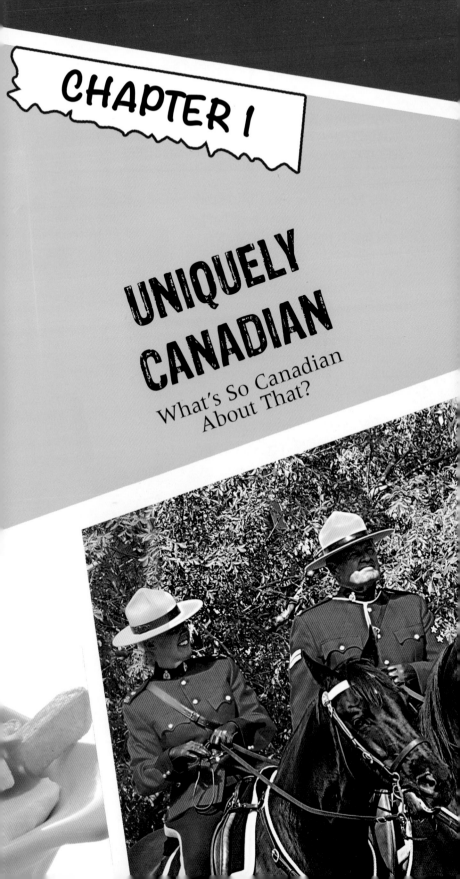

INUKSUK
Pointing the way

YOU'RE IN THE COLD, TREELESS ARCTIC, LOST AND ALONE. SUDDENLY YOU SEE A TALL STANDING STONE STRUCTURE. YOU GO THE DIRECTION THE ARMS POINT AND, TO YOUR RELIEF, FIND WARMTH AND SHELTER.

Who Made the First Inuksuk?

These stone statues have been built and used by the Inuit and other people living in the Arctic region of North America for centuries. The word *inuksuk* is made up of two Inuit words: *inuk* = man and *suk* = substitute. But *inuksuit* (plural for inuksuk) don't just tell travellers which way to go; they also mark fishing spots, hunting grounds or spots where food is stored. In a landscape with few natural landmarks, they've helped countless travellers over thousands of years.

Enukso Point on Baffin Island has over 100 inuksuit and in 1969 it was designated a historic site.

Today

The inuksuk continues to be a beloved symbol of Canada. Inuksuit inspired the design of the Vancouver 2010 Olympic logo. The inuksuk logo was chosen for its simple, welcoming look, well-suited to the spirit of the games and Vancouver.

WOULD YOU BELIEVE . . . ?

In July 2005 the Canadian military erected an inuksuk on Hans Island, a small Arctic island. The statue was to mark Canada's claim over the island in a long-standing dispute with Denmark.

HUDSON'S BAY POINT BLANKET
The point is: stay warm

THE POINT BLANKET IS A UNIQUE CANADIAN ICON THAT ORIGINATED IN THE EIGHTEENTH CENTURY AND IS STILL POPULAR TODAY.

Not Just Any Blanket

In 1780, fur trader Monsieur Germain Maugenest suggested that the Hudson's Bay Company produce "point" blankets for trade. The company followed Maugenest's advice and was soon busy trading blankets to Aboriginal peoples for beaver pelts, buffalo robes, moccasins and other goods. These now-iconic blankets had green, red, yellow and indigo stripes on a white background. The Aboriginal peoples loved the cozy wool blankets to sleep under and wear, for their warmth and ability to hold heat even when wet.

Great coats!

What's the Point?

The "point" in the blanket's name was a system used by French fur-trading companies dating back to the mid 1700s. The points are the thin black lines that are woven into each blanket. The number of points notes the blanket's size and weight. The larger and heavier the blanket, the more it was worth.

**WOULD Y
BELIEVE . .**
The most common use
point blankets was in t
making of capotes, the fam
blanket coats shown in the
picture above.

Still Going Strong

Many early point blankets have survived into the twenty-first century and have become highly sought-after collectibles. They fetch thousands of dollars at auction today. The Hudson's Bay Company continues to make blankets and coats for people all over Canada and beyond. The popular signature stripes are also used on bed linens, shirts, belts, shopping bags and umbrellas.

TUQUES AND MUKLUKS
Cozy from head to toes

OUR ANCESTORS KNEW THAT STAYING WARM IN A CANADIAN WINTER STARTS WITH A WARM HEAD AND ENDS WITH TOASTY TOES.

What's on Top?

How do you keep your head and ears warm on a wintery day? You put on a tuque! The word *tuque* and the design of this brimless cap began with French Canadian fur traders back in the 1800s. But the word was in use even earlier. Some say it's related to an Italian word, *tocca*, which means "cap." Others contend that it refers to an ancient pre-Roman term meaning "hill" or "gourd." That makes sense: a tuque looks like a knitted hill on your head.

Wherever it began, it's Canadian now. Go anywhere else in the world and say "tuque" and they're unlikely to know what you're talking about.

WOULD YOU BELIEVE . . . ?
There's a town in Quebec called La Tuque. The hill there looks like — you guessed it — a tuque!

Toasty Toes

Mukluks have a long history of treading on Canadian land. The Yupik and other Aboriginal peoples used seal, moose or caribou to make these soft, up-to-the-mid-calf boots that could withstand the freezing conditions of the North. The earliest mukluks were lined with bear, squirrel or beaver fur. They were worn when fishing, hunting, walking in snowshoes or travelling by canoe. It took hours of careful work to make each pair.

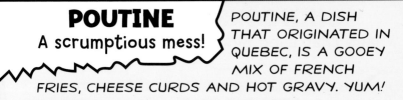

POUTINE
A scrumptious mess!

POUTINE, A DISH THAT ORIGINATED IN QUEBEC, IS A GOOEY MIX OF FRENCH FRIES, CHEESE CURDS AND HOT GRAVY. YUM!

Who Invented It?

"I wanted fries but I saw cheese curds on the counter so I asked Fernand to mix them together." That's what customer Eddie Lanaisse recalls telling Quebec restaurateur Fernand LaChance in 1957. What was LaChance's reply? "That's going to make a mess!" Despite his reservations, LaChance prepared the "mess" and it caught on. In 1964 he added hot gravy to the dish to melt the curds. That's how one story goes about the origin of poutine.

Restaurateur Jean-Paul Roy also claims to have invented poutine in 1964 when *he* added gravy to the fries and curds. Whatever its origins, poutine has become an increasingly popular dish. You can now find it in many restaurants — from fast food chains to fancy spots — and even trendy food trucks across Canada and beyond.

Tasty, yes. But, healthy? Not so much. A serving of poutine can add 1,000 calories to your diet!

WOULD YOU BELIEVE . . . ?
Curds, bits of cheese coated with a thick layer of milk, have to be fresh to be good. If they're not, you don't get the special "squeak," the sound a good curd makes when you bite into it.

How Do You Take Your Poutine?

Today poutine might include unusual ingredients like meatballs, fried chicken, lobster and even foie gras (the fattened liver of a duck or goose). An Asian version might include lemon grass, red chili and coconut cream. Whatever the combination, and despite the fatty ingredients and messy look, poutine lovers keep coming back for more.

CHINOOKS
What's that wind blowing in?

IF YOU'RE FREEZING IN YOUR THICK PARKA ONE MINUTE AND SHEDDING IT TO JOG IN YOUR SHORTS THE NEXT, WHERE ARE YOU? PROBABLY IN SOUTHERN ALBERTA IN WINTER, AND A CHINOOK WIND IS PASSING THROUGH!

Why the Dramatic Shift?

A chinook is a warm, usually dry wind that can cause a big change in winter temperatures. The winds start from the wet Pacific coast. They cool down as they climb the western slopes of the Rocky Mountains and quickly warm as they descend the eastern slopes. There's a sudden change in the speed and direction of the wind. The gusty winds bring temperatures up quickly. The strong, warm winds also carry sound long distances and make for gorgeous sunsets.

It's Not All Good

Despite the pleasant warmth after a day of biting cold, there are downsides to chinooks. The sudden dryness brings an increased risk of fire. Some delicate trees, like the white birch, become damaged. Leaves sprout in the warmth and then drop off in the next frost. Snow cover can be lost, robbing plants of moisture. Animals get confused and may stumble in the thin layer of ice. Some people get terrible headaches or feel depressed. But many just welcome the break from winter.

WOULD YOU BELIEVE . . . ?

On January 11, 1983, a chinook blew through Calgary, Alberta, and the temperature rose 30°C in four hours. In February 1992, a chinook caused Claresholme, Alberta, to hit 24°C — one of Canada's highest February temperatures.

"Those who have not the warm invigorating chinook winds of this country cannot well comprehend what a blessing they are. The icy clutch of winter is lessened."
— *Calgary Herald,* turn of the 20th century

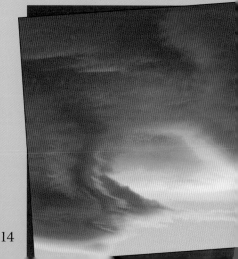

THERE'S NOTHING LIKE PADDLING A KAYAK DOWN A RIVER, ON A LAKE OR IN THE SEA. YOU GLIDE, RIDE THE WAVES, FISH, EXPLORE A HIDDEN COVE OR JUST ENJOY A DAY OUT.

Who Built It First?

An early version of the kayak, the *umiak*, was a large, skin-covered, wood-frame, open boat that was probably built and designed on the cold coast of Siberia thousands of years ago. When people in Siberia migrated to the Americas about 10,000 to 15,000 years ago, they brought their umiaks with them.

Then Came the Kayak

The Inuit of the Arctic used umiaks, like the one above, to transport people, material and dogs long distances. About 4,000 years ago when the Inuit ventured farther into the ocean to hunt, they designed the kayak. With its covered deck and leaner lines, the kayak was better at navigating the open sea. These early kayaks were made of seal or other animal skins stretched over a wood or whalebone frame. Seal oil was rubbed on for waterproofing. Most kayaks today are made of moulded polyethylene resins.

> Kayak means "man's boat" or "hunter's boat." Women more often travelled in umiaks.

LACROSSE
The official summer sport

FIND A LARGE FIELD. ORGANIZE TWO TEAMS WITH TEN PLAYERS EACH. GIVE THEM LONG-HANDLED STICKS WITH WEBBED POUCHES, AND A RUBBER BALL, THEN PLAY!

Who Invented Lacrosse?

One of the oldest team sports in North America, lacrosse originated with First Nations, probably in the seventeenth century, as a way to settle inter-tribal disputes, to strengthen warriors for combat, for religious purposes, for fun or as part of a festival. It was played all over Canada, but was most popular around the Great Lakes.

At games, medicine men were coaches, and the women served refreshments.

How Was It Played?

The games sometimes lasted for days, and could be played by as many as 100 to 1,000 men from opposing villages. They would often start at sunrise and end at sunset. There were special dances and ceremonies. Bets were placed and players decorated their bodies and sticks.

The balls were made of wood, or deerskin stuffed with hair. The first sticks were like giant spoons, with no netting. The game started when a ball was tossed in the air and players rushed to catch it.

Westerners Get in the Game

Although Jesuit missionaries disapproved of the betting and violence, a Jesuit priest, Jean de Brébeuf, is thought to have been the first to write about lacrosse. Soon French colonists were playing too. In 1856, a dentist, William George Beers, founded the Montreal Lacrosse Club. In the 1860s, it became the national game.

There are four types played here today: men's and women's field lacrosse, box lacrosse (played indoors, with six players per team) and inter-crosse (designed for school and recreation programs).

MOUNTED POLICE
Keeping Canada safe

WHAT DO CRISP SCARLET UNIFORMS, STETSON HATS, STATELY HORSES AND SMART DOGS HAVE IN COMMON? THEY'RE ALL PART OF THE ROYAL CANADIAN MOUNTED POLICE FORCE.

A New Force

In May 1873, Parliament established a police force for the North-West Territories (present-day Alberta and Saskatchewan), the North West Mounted Police. That year 150 recruits took off for the West, to establish and supervise law and order among the fur and whiskey traders and the Aboriginal people, as well as the Americans to the south.

Sam Steele

A legendary member of the NWMP, Sam Steele led new recruits on their gruelling March West in 1874. In the 1880s he played a key role policing the construction of the Canadian Pacific Railway, quelling the Rebellion of 1885 (a Métis uprising under Louis Riel against the government of Canada), restoring order in Kootenay after tensions rose between the white and First Nations people, and maintaining peace during the 1898 Yukon gold rush.

A New Name

In 1920 the NWMP merged with the Dominion Police to become the Royal Canadian Mounted Police. The RCMP is headquartered in Regina, Manitoba.

Today the force combats organized crime, terrorism and the spread of drugs, performs VIP and airport security, and much more.

PEMMICAN AND BANNOCK
Food on the go

WHAT WERE THE FIRST CANADIAN DISHES? THESE HIGHLY NUTRITIOUS FOODS PROVIDED SUSTENANCE FOR ABORIGINAL PEOPLES AND THE EUROPEAN EXPLORERS WHO LEARNED FROM THEM.

Who Made it First?

Did someone pack the pemmican?

What's a nutritious, high-energy food that travels well and became a favourite of famous explorers? Pemmican! Pemmican was first made by the Aboriginal peoples of North America. European explorers, like Alexander Mackenzie (right), Samuel Hearne and Roald Amundsen, adopted it too, as it was perfect for long journeys. The word *pemmican* means "grease" or "fat" in Cree.

Recipe for Perfect Pemmican

Thinly slice your meat (usually bison or buffalo but elk, moose or deer are used too) and dry it in the sun or over a slow fire until it's hard. Pound it into small pieces, mix with hot fat and add dried fruit like Saskatoon berries or cranberries to spark up the flavour. Store as long as you want.

Bannock for Everyone

Bannock is a flat cake, also known as fried bread, trail bread, bush bread and grease bread. First Nations peoples made it from ingredients gathered in the woods, such as seeds, nuts, flour from roots and the syrup from tree sap — and served it with freshly caught fish.

When Europeans arrived in Canada, they brought wheat flour and made bannock with that. The Scots, who'd been cooking their version for centuries, often used oats, rye or barley flour.

"Too much cannot be said of the importance of pemmican to a polar expedition." — North Pole explorer Robert Peary

18

SNOWSHOES AND GOGGLES
Tramping through the snow

NO BIG SURPRISE: THOSE WHO EXPERIENCED THIS COUNTRY FIRST INVENTED NIFTY WAYS OF DEALING WITH SNOW.

The Snowshoe Story

Each Aboriginal community developed its own style of snowshoes to suit its climate, terrain and needs. The Inuit made snowshoes good for trekking through deep, powdery snow. More southerly tribes, like the Cree, developed narrower and longer snowshoes to manoeuvre easily through the forest.

In the eighteenth and nineteenth centuries, French Canadian voyageurs and coureurs de bois adapted snowshoes to travel and trap animals in the wilderness. In the 1840s, a group of businessmen founded the Montreal Snow Shoe Club. Snowshoe clubs grew for many years through the 1800s. In the 1890s, skating and hockey took over as more popular winter sports.

> ### WOULD YOU BELIEVE . . . ?
> On March 13, 1758, during the French and Indian War, British Rangers fought wearing snowshoes in a battle called The Battle of Snowshoe. The British lost the battle.

And Don't Forget the Eyes

The Aboriginal peoples in the Arctic came up with the world's first sunglasses — to shield their eyes from snow blindness. Snow goggles originated over 2,000 years ago with the ancestors of the Inuit, who brought them to Canada more than 800 years ago. The goggles were crafted of bone, leather or wood and had small slits to see through.

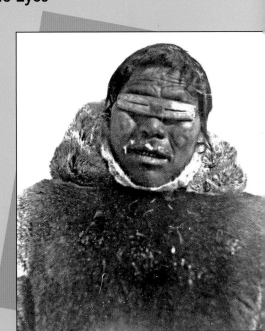

Canada is the second-largest country in the world, but it's in top place when it comes to being awesome! It also has the world's longest coastline, and some of the most extreme weather and weirdest animals. If you're extreme-ly interested, keep reading.

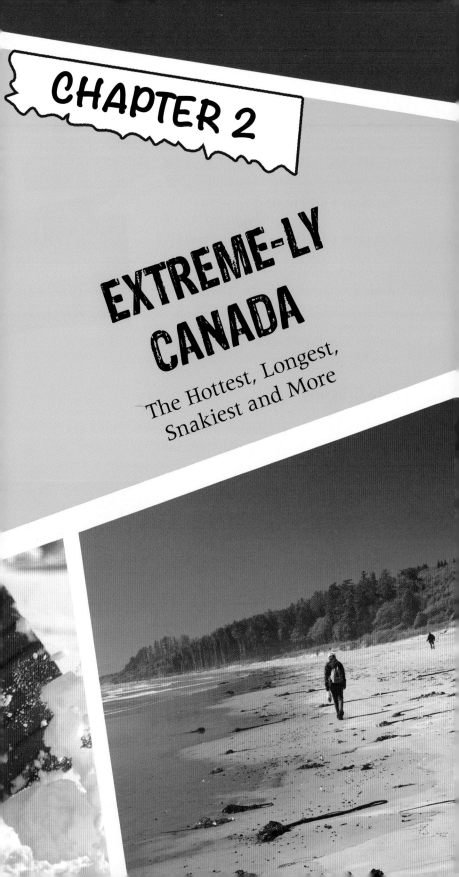

CHAPTER 2

EXTREME-LY CANADA

The Hottest, Longest, Snakiest and More

THE SNAKIEST
Slithering, sliding, slipping, slinking

IF YOU LIKE SNAKES, THEN YOU'VE GOT TO VISIT THE SNAKE PITS OUTSIDE OF NARCISSE, MANITOBA. YOU CAN SEE MORE SNAKES HERE THAN ANYWHERE ELSE IN THE WORLD.

Rustling and Hissing

Lissss-ten up!

Not only will you see the snakes — you'll hear them too! As tens of thousands of red-sided garter snakes slither over one another in huge tangled heaps, their scales rub together to make a constant, rustling hiss.

The snakes spend the winter underground in crevasses and caverns. In the spring, they emerge from their dens to mate. They form mating balls made up of one female and as many as 100 males.

Safe Crossing

To travel to and from their winter dens, the snakes have to cross a highway. You can guess what happens when snakes and cars collide. Yuck! So snake lovers have built tunnels under the roadway. Fences guide the snakes into the tunnels so they can cross safely.

Sssssee You Later

Like most Canadian snakes, these garter snakes avoid humans. There are only a few venomous snakes in the country and they like to be left alone, too. Snake bites are rare in Canada, but any wild animal may bite if it feels threatened. Snakes are actually great animals to have around, especially in gardens, since they eat grubs, snails, leeches and other pests.

WOULD YOU BELIEVE . . . ?

Canada has the world's largest populations of a few other animals too:
- The biggest caribou (also called reindeer) herd, in Canada's North.
- The world's largest herd of wood bison, in Wood Buffalo National Park (on the border of Alberta and the Northwest Territories).
- And let's not forget Vancouver Island marmots — because our country is the only place where this little gopher-like animal is found!

WEATHER HIGHS AND LOWS
Hot, cold, snowy and sunny

WHATEVER THE WEATHER, CANADA'S GOT IT, IN EXTREMES.

Hottest and Coldest

If you love the heat, head to Alberta. On July 28, 1903, the temperature in Gleichen, Alberta, hit 46°C — the highest temperature ever recorded in Canada. And Manyberries, in southeastern Alberta, is the country's sunniest spot.

In 1947, the temperature in Snag, Yukon, dropped to –63°C, the lowest temperature ever in Canada *and* North America. That's about the same temperature as the icy drifts of Mars!

WOULD YOU BELIEVE . . . ?
Every year, experts estimate that about 1 septillion snowflakes fall on Canada. That's 1,000,000,000,000,000, 000,000,000!

Wettest and Driest

Prince Rupert, British Columbia, receives about 2,594 millimetres of rain each year. That's more than any other Canadian city. Canada's driest place is in B.C. too — Ashcroft gets just 200 millimetres of rain and snow every year.

Snowiest and Hail-iest

St. John's, Newfoundland, received 68.4 centimetres of snow on April 5, 1999. That would bury you up to about your waist! And Calgary has had a snowstorm every month of the year — even July and August!

On August 27, 1973, Canada's largest hailstone ever fell near Cedoux, Saskatchewan. It measured 11 centimetres in diameter, or bigger than a softball. Ouch! In September 1991 a hailstorm hit the Calgary area and caused $400 million worth of damage.

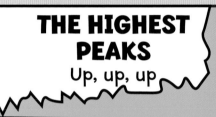

THE HIGHEST PEAKS
Up, up, up

IF YOU WANT TO CLIMB CANADA'S HIGHEST MOUNTAIN THEN YOU HAVE TO HEAD UP — UP NORTH, THAT IS.

From Peak . . .

Mount Logan is located in southwestern Yukon and at 5,959 metres tall, there's only one higher peak in all of North America. And Mount Logan is still getting taller, thanks to the way the Earth shifts and moves. Mount Logan is extreme in a few other ways. Of all the mountains in the world that didn't start out as volcanoes, Mount Logan is the biggest around at its base. And with its high winds, Mount Logan is one of the coldest places on Earth.

. . . to Peak

The Rocky Mountains are Canada's most famous mountains, and they also stretch down into the United States. In the Canadian Rockies, the highest peak is Mount Robson, which towers 3,954 metres tall.

There are many peaks in the Rockies higher than the one called Snow Dome, but that mountain stands out for another reason. Water flowing off the top of it can go in three directions: to the Pacific Ocean, the Arctic Ocean or the Atlantic Ocean (through Hudson Bay). There's no other point like that in North America.

Lucky I'm not afraid of heights!

THE FARTHEST POINTS

CANADA IS NORTH OF THE UNITED STATES, RIGHT?

NOT ALWAYS. MORE THAN HALF (27) OF THE AMERICAN STATES ARE AT LEAST PARTLY NORTH OF CANADA'S MOST SOUTHERN POINT, AND 13 ARE COMPLETELY NORTH OF IT.

North to South

Canada's (and North America's) most northerly point is Cape Aldrich, just 987 kilometres south of the North Pole. Nobody lives there permanently, so to visit the northernmost spot where people live, head to Alert, Nunavut. No town in the entire world is farther north than Alert — which makes it home to the world's northernmost bowling alley.

And what is Canada's southernmost point? It's Middle Island, in Lake Erie in southern Ontario, part of Point Pelee National Park.

East to West

Every morning, the sun rises in Cape Spear, Newfoundland, before anywhere else in Canada — or North America. For Canada's westernmost point, you have to head north again, all the way up to the border of Yukon and Alaska.

In the Middle

Where's the middle of Canada? In Manitoba or Ontario? Take another look at a map — it's actually all the way up in southeastern Nunavut, near Yathkyed Lake.

WOULD YOU BELIEVE . . . ?

Some of Canada's parks are bigger than entire countries. For instance, Wood Buffalo National Park (between Alberta and the Northwest Territories) is bigger than Denmark or Switzerland. Nahanni National Park Reserve in the Northwest Territories is larger than Albania or Israel.

BIG WATER
Remarkable rivers, limitless lakes

CANADA HAS ABOUT THREE MILLION LAKES, MORE THAN THE REST OF THE WORLD COMBINED!

The Biggest

Great Bear Lake is the biggest lake that's entirely in Canada. Since it is located in the Northwest Territories, you won't be surprised to discover that it's at least partially frozen for two-thirds of every year. The lake is named after the Chipewyan First Nation who lived on the north shores — Chipewyan means "grizzly bear water people."

Look Ma, I'm a lake!

The Deepest

Not only is Great Slave Lake Canada's deepest lake, it's also North America's. This lake gets its name from the Slavey First Nation who live in the area. Legends are told of a huge dragon-headed monster that lives down in the depths of the lake.

Biggest of All

Bigger than both of these lakes is Lake Superior, one of the Great Lakes, in Ontario. It straddles Canada's border with the United States, so it isn't entirely in Canada. But it covers more area than any other freshwater lake in the world.

The Longest

When it comes to rivers, the Mackenzie River is Canada's largest and longest. It mostly flows through the Northwest Territories, and it runs north to the Arctic Ocean. With its tributaries, the smaller rivers that run into it, the Mackenzie is one of the longest rivers in the world.

WOULD YOU BELIEVE . . . ?
There's enough water in Lake Superior to cover both North and South America with 30 centimetres of water.

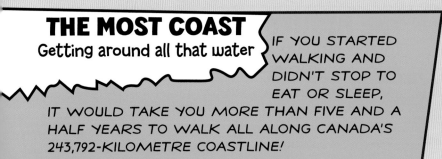

THE MOST COAST
Getting around all that water

IF YOU STARTED WALKING AND DIDN'T STOP TO EAT OR SLEEP, IT WOULD TAKE YOU MORE THAN FIVE AND A HALF YEARS TO WALK ALL ALONG CANADA'S 243,792-KILOMETRE COASTLINE!

Shoreline Bragging Rights

Don't forget to bring along a change of shoes — and boots — when you head out on that walk. Some of Canada's coastline is sandy and warm, but a lot of it is rocky, and some is frozen all year round.

When it comes to shoreline, Canada takes the gold medal by a long shot. No other country even comes close — it's almost five times as long as the silver medalist's (Indonesia's) total. It's hard to believe, but Canada's coastline is more than six times as long as the distance around Earth's equator.

Why So Much Coast?

Not only does our country border the Atlantic, Arctic and Pacific oceans, but we also have the shorelines of our 52,455 islands. Another reason is that no bay in the world has a longer shoreline than Canada's Hudson Bay. Named after explorer Henry Hudson, this bay that dips down into the middle of the country is huge. Despite its size, Hudson Bay has only about a dozen villages scattered along its lengthy coast.

Newfoundland and Labrador has the most coast, at 28,956 kilometres, including its islands. Alberta and Saskatchewan have none at all.

THE HIGHEST TIDE
In and out, up and down

NOWHERE IN THE WORLD ARE THE TIDES HIGHER THAN IN CANADA. TWO CANADIAN PLACES CLAIM THE TITLE FOR THE HIGHEST TIDES ON THE PLANET.

Hi, Tide!

Several times a day, the levels of the world's oceans rise and fall. These high tides and low tides are caused by the pull of the moon and the sun, as well as Earth's rotation.

Most people think the world's highest tides happen at the Bay of Fundy, which separates New Brunswick and Nova Scotia. On average, the difference between low tide and high tide is an incredible 17 metres.

Scientists say the high tides are caused by the speed of the waves and the V-shape of the Bay of Fundy, which funnels the water from the wide mouth at the ocean into less and less space. Mi'kmaq First Nation legends tell stories about how these high tides are caused by a giant whale.

It's a Tide Tie!

Tied with the Bay of Fundy for the world's highest tides is Ungava Bay, at the top of Quebec, just below Baffin Island. Like the Maritime bay, Ungava Bay is V-shaped.

It's important to know about tides because they affect where and when fishing boats and other ships can safely sail. As well, tides affect how bridges and docks are built.

WOULD YOU BELIEVE . . . ?

The Bay of Fundy's Hopewell Rocks, also known as the "flowerpot" rocks, are best seen at low tide, as above. Flip to page 66 to see how they look at high tide. The rocks' strange shape is caused by the tides, which have worn away the bottoms more than the tops.

FORESTS, FORESTS EVERYWHERE
It's tree-rific!

THERE ARE FEW COUNTRIES IN THE WORLD THAT HAVE MORE FORESTS THAN CANADA. YOU'LL FIND ABOUT 10% OF THE WORLD'S FORESTS IN OUR COUNTRY.

Have You Hugged a Tree Today?

More than half of Canada is covered with boreal forests, northern forests where you'll find mostly evergreen trees such as cedar, pine and spruce. Trees are vital to the life of our planet! They produce oxygen, which we need to breathe.

Trees also improve our environment by absorbing noise and filtering pollution out of rain water. In winter, trees provide windbreaks for people and animals, and in summer their shade cools the air. Tree roots prevent soil from washing away in rains.

This one's mine!

The Giants

British Columbia is the home of the world's tallest Douglas fir. Vancouver Island's Red Creek Douglas Fir towers 74 metres tall, or more than 24 stories high. This giant is greater than 4 metres across. Experts figure it took more than 1,000 years for the tree to grow so huge.

But the tallest tree in Canada is probably the Carmanah Giant Sitka Spruce. Also located on Vancouver Island, it soars 95 metres high, making it taller than a 30-storey building, and possibly the tallest Sitka Spruce in the world!

WOULD YOU BELIEVE . . . ?
Vancouver Island is home to many of Canada's tallest trees. That's because they get lots of light, food and water there. They also have to grow tall to reach for sunlight.

Canadian provinces hold down eight of the top ten spots for provinces and states with the most forests.

THE STRANGEST ANIMALS
Teeth, nose and naps

THE WORLD'S STRANGEST ANIMALS? WE'VE GOT OUR SHARE OF THEM. HERE ARE SOME THAT TAKE THE PRIZE.

Unicorn of the Sea

Unicorns are the stuff of legends, but this creature is real. The narwhal has a horn — it's actually a tooth — that can can grow as long as 2.7 metres. Males sometimes battle with their horns, like a sword fight.

> ### WOULD YOU BELIEVE . . . ?
> A reindeer's eye colour changes from deep blue in the winter to yellow in the summer. This helps it see well in both the low light of winter and the bright light of summer.

A Real Star

No animal has a more complex or sensitive snout than the star-nosed mole. It uses the 22 tentacles on its nose to find food. It can identify and eat food in just 120 milliseconds!

A Cold Winter Napper

Over the winter, the wood frog burrows underground. As the soil freezes, so do the frog's brain, eyes and heart. When spring comes, the frog defrosts and is soon hopping about again.

Sea scorpions living in Canada 400 million years ago were as big as cars.

THE MOST DANGEROUS ANIMALS
Caution: scary creatures ahead

WHO'S THE SCARIEST OF ALL? THE ANSWERS MAY SURPRISE YOU.

Luckily, They Don't Like Us

What do you think are Canada's scariest creatures? Bears? Wolves? Cougars? It's true that all of these can be extremely dangerous, thanks to their strength, sharp teeth and deadly claws. But most of these animals keep far away from where people live. Canada has a few venomous snakes, too, but rather than sink their teeth into you, they usually slither off into the grass so you never even know they're nearby.

Shy Spider, Nice Spider

The brown recluse spider, also known as a fiddleback spider because of the violin-shaped markings on its body, can kill with its bite. Luckily, this spider tends to live where it won't be disturbed, so few people are ever bitten by one.

Watch who you're calling itsy-bitsy.

Give Them Space

They don't have sharp teeth or claws, but elk and moose can cause a lot of damage because of their size and weight. They're not afraid of humans, they're often involved in car accidents and they can be very aggressive in mating season or when they have babies to protect.

WOULD YOU BELIEVE . . . ?
Which animals do the most damage to humans? Dogs, horses and cows — mostly because so many people spend so much time near them. And mosquitoes can be very dangerous if they're carrying the West Nile virus, a serious illness.

Moo?

31

So much has happened in Canada since its four colonies joined together in 1867. Canada has expanded to ten provinces and three territories. It now stretches from the Atlantic to the Pacific and way up north to the Arctic. It has built a transcontinental railway, discovered oil, hosted three Olympics and celebrated a champion racing ship. Read on and discover the stories behind ten unforgettable and nation-shaping events.

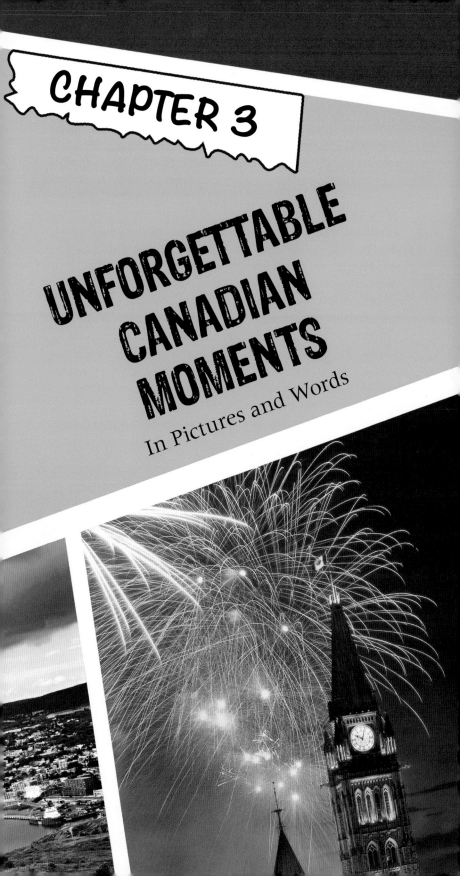

CHAPTER 3

UNFORGETTABLE CANADIAN MOMENTS

In Pictures and Words

HAPPY BIRTHDAY, CANADA!
Confederation unites the provinces

ON JULY 1, 1867, WITH THE BRITISH NORTH AMERICA ACT, BRITISH PARLIAMENT OFFICIALLY UNITED NOVA SCOTIA, NEW BRUNSWICK, QUEBEC AND ONTARIO AS THE DOMINION OF CANADA.

Why Unite?
• **Politics**: The province of Canada (now Ontario and Quebec) had the most people, but the English- and French-speaking halves didn't always agree. Joining the other colonies might help fix their own political problems.

• **Economics**: Canada exported a lot of goods to Britain, like fish, timber and furs. But Britain started buying elsewhere, too. Strengthening trade *within* Canada was smart.

• **Security**: The colonies worried the United States could buy or take Canadian land. After all, they'd acquired the Oregon territory from Britain in 1846 and seized Texas from Mexico. And in 1812, they did try to invade Canada.

• **Transportation:** The promise of a railway linking Canada was enticing for travel and trade, and would be more easily realized by a united country working together.

"Let us be French, let us be English, but most importantly let us be Canadian!"
— John A. Macdonald, Canada's first prime minister

Who Joined When?
It took 132 years for all the parts of Canada to get on board.
1867: New Brunswick, Nova Scotia, Ontario, Quebec
1870: Manitoba, Northwest Territories
1871: British Columbia
1873: Prince Edward Island
1898: Yukon
1905: Alberta, Saskatchewan
1949: Newfoundland and Labrador
1999: Nunavut

THE LAST SPIKE
From sea to sea by rail

ON NOVEMBER 7, 1885, A GROUP OF CANADIAN PACIFIC RAILWAY EXECUTIVES, BUILDERS AND SURVEYORS MET IN CRAIGELLACHIE, BRITISH COLUMBIA, TO CELEBRATE AN ASTONISHING FEAT: THE BUILDING OF A RAILWAY LINKING CANADA.

Not Finished Yet!

Although the ceremony was held to celebrate the completion of the railway, there was still more work to be done to make regular service available.

WOULD YOU BELIEVE . . . ?

Donald Smith, who provided financing and support for the railway, was given the honour of hammering in the last spike. Unfortunately his first attempt bent the spike. But on his second try he drove a spike in, as the famous photo (at right) shows.

How Did They Do It?

All you have to do is look at a map of Canada and you can see how hard it would be to build a railway through such a vast country with so many different terrains. The job required engineering feats and a lot of backbreaking, dangerous work.

The West had almost impassable mountains and workers had to use dynamite to blast their way through.

Many workers' lives were lost, but in the end the railway was built. It became a political and economic unifying force in Canada.

TITANIC RESCUE
Halifax helps out

ON THE COLD NIGHT OF APRIL 14, 1912, WORD ARRIVED AT THE CAPE RACE MARCONI STATION IN NEWFOUNDLAND THAT THE MAGNIFICENT OCEAN LINER TITANIC HIT AN ICEBERG 590 KILOMETRES SOUTHEAST OF NEWFOUNDLAND.

Nightmare at Sea

The telegraph said the passengers were safe and the ship would soon be towed to Halifax. It wasn't long before the world learned the terrible truth. The White Star Line's "unsinkable" *Titanic* had gone down in only 2 hours and 40 minutes.

More than 1,500 passengers perished. After drifting in lifeboats in the frigid ocean for hours, just over 700 survivors were finally picked up by the rescue ship *Carpathia*. Soon after, four vessels were dispatched from Halifax to recover bodies from the wreckage.

Halifax Remembers

You can still visit the graves of *Titanic* victims at Fairview Lawn Cemetery in Halifax, and learn the story of the ship and the role that Halifax played at the Maritime Museum of the Atlantic. The museum houses many rare artifacts such as a child's shoe, a button and a deck chair. They were retrieved from the bottom of the ocean after Dr. Robert Ballard and his crew, including Canadian researcher Joseph MacInnis, discovered the remains of the ship in 1985.

A Blockbuster Movie

Canadian director James Cameron's 1997 movie *Titanic* won many awards, including an Academy Award for best picture. It also used groundbreaking remotely operated vehicle technology to film the actual shipwreck for the epic movie.

WOULD YOU BELIEVE . . . ?
Hilda Slayter, a *Titanic* passenger and native of Halifax, miraculously survived not only the shipwreck but also the Halifax Explosion five years later. Now that's luck!

BLUENOSE WAS A LEGENDARY FISHING AND RACING SCHOONER, WHICH STILL HOLDS A SPECIAL PLACE IN THE HEARTS OF MARITIMERS.

Built for Speed

Bluenose launched in Lunenburg, Nova Scotia, on March 26, 1921. Speed matters for fishing vessels — the first back to port get the best price for their catch. This sleek vessel, captained by Angus Walters, defeated her American rival, *Elsie*, in the International Fisherman's Trophy Race that October. *Bluenose* went on to win many more international racing awards, and continued to be a hard-working fishing boat, plying the waters for cod and other fish.

Changing Times

In the 1930s, motorized boats and trawlers replaced fishing schooners. *Bluenose* was sold as a freighter to the West Indian Trading Company. On January 28, 1946, laden with bananas, she struck a reef off Haiti and went down.

The Legend Continues

Despite her sad end, the schooner's legacy carries on. An image of *Bluenose* is on Nova Scotia licence plates, has been on the dime since 1937 and has appeared on three postage stamps.

In 1963, a replica of *Bluenose* was built using the original plans. In 1971, *Bluenose II* was gifted to the Canadian government. The schooner sails around North America, and people can come on board to experience this piece of maritime history.

WE STRUCK OIL
Black gold in Leduc, Alberta!

FEBRUARY 13, 1947: EVERYONE PRESENT WATCHED IN AMAZEMENT AS OIL GUSHED OUT OF THE GROUND IN LEDUC, ALBERTA. ALBERTA WAS NEVER THE SAME AGAIN.

Drilling for Oil

For years there were rumours of rich oil deposits in Alberta. Aboriginal peoples used what seemed like oil to waterproof their canoes, and as a medicinal ointment. In the late nineteenth century pioneers noted a film on pools of water and a strange smell in the air. It had to be oil!

In 1913, drilling began and three wells did produce oil. In no time, 500 oil companies were formed but many were out to con eager investors. As for oil, what was generally found was naphtha, a type of natural gas. Over the following years, despite a few successful drills, most failed.

Last Chance Drill

After so many failures, companies and investors were ready to give up. The Imperial Oil company decided to try one more time. A team began drilling on a farm 15 kilometres west of Leduc. To everyone's astonishment, a test drill sent up a geyser of oil. On February 13, 1947, the real drilling began. The ground rumbled, the crowd held their breath and oil gushed out of the well known as Leduc No. 1.

Oil Changes Alberta

Oil brought prosperity and a population boom to Alberta. Today, Alberta is full of refineries, petrochemical plants, pipeline companies and oil-related businesses. Alberta went from being a "have-not" province to being a rich and self-sufficient one.

WOULD YOU BELIEVE . . . ?

Before the Leduc strike, Imperial Oil had spent millions and drilled 133 consecutive dry wells in Alberta and Saskatchewan over a 27-year period in search of oil.

NEWFOUNDLAND JOINS CANADA
At long last

IT TOOK MORE THAN 80 YEARS AND A COUPLE OF REFERENDUMS, BUT FINALLY, IN 1949, NEWFOUNDLAND BECAME CANADA'S NEWEST PROVINCE.

What Took So Long?

Newfoundlanders liked being independent. They felt they could thrive on their own, so while many former British colonies chose to become part of Canada in 1867, Newfoundland refused.

Tough Times Change Minds

In the 1920s, the fishing industry declined rapidly and Newfoundland's economy suffered badly. By the 1930s, with the Great Depression, the economy got even worse.

World War II brought American bases, troops and prosperity to Newfoundland but many worried about what would happen after the war. After all, Britain was short on money and busy rebuilding itself. The English wouldn't be keen on helping Newfoundland's faltering economy. At the same time, Canada worried that the United States would have too much influence in Newfoundland. The time was ripe to reconsider.

Joey Smallwood Speaks Up

Joey Smallwood, a journalist and radio host, pushed hard to encourage Newfoundland to join Canada — to improve public services, standards and trade. In 1948, two referendums were held in Newfoundland to decide what its people wanted to do about joining Canada. The vote was a "Yes" to joining Canada, by a majority of 52.3%. Joey Smallwood was soon elected Newfoundland's first premier.

In 2001, the province's name was officially changed from Newfoundland to Newfoundland and Labrador.

A FLAG OF OUR OWN
Red, white and maple

THE OFFICIAL NATIONAL FLAG OF CANADA, A LARGE RED MAPLE LEAF SET ON A BACKGROUND OF WHITE WITH RED BORDERS, WAS UNFURLED AND FLOWN ON FEBRUARY 15, 1965.

The Great Flag Debate

It took over forty years to design and approve a Canadian flag! A committee first began researching designs in 1925. Another committee was created in 1946, and more than 2,600 suggestions were received, some of which are shown below. But the committee could not agree. In 1964, as Canada's centennial year approached, the push for a flag heated up. Finally, the eye-catching, attractive maple leaf design by Dr. George Stanley of the Royal Military College in Kingston was approved by Parliament. Canada finally had a flag.

Why This Design?

A flag brings people together and reminds them what's unique about their country. What's behind ours? Red and white have represented France and England throughout history. They were approved as Canada's official colours in 1921 by King George V. The maple tree had long been important to the Aboriginal peoples who gathered sap every spring. The maple leaf as a symbol of the country can be traced back as early as 1700.

The flag design reflected the goal of representing all Canadians "without distinction of race, language, belief and opinion."

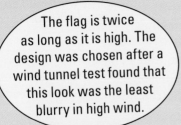

The flag is twice as long as it is high. The design was chosen after a wind tunnel test found that this look was the least blurry in high wind.

40

A NEW TERRITORY IS BORN
Welcome, Nunavut!

ON APRIL 1, 1999, NUNAVUT WAS BORN AS A CANADIAN TERRITORY. PARTIES, SPEECHES, TRADITIONAL INUIT GAMES AND DANCES CELEBRATED THE EVENT.

A Long History

The Tuniit (Dorset) people were the first to inhabit Nunavut and are believed to have crossed from Russia via the land bridge (now the Bering Strait) about 5,000 years ago. About 1,000 years ago, the Thule people showed up in the area, and eventually became the dominant culture. The Inuit, descendants of the Thule, began trading with Basque and Portuguese whalers in the 1500s and came into contact with European explorers seeking the Northwest Passage. Despite all this, Inuit life didn't change much.

Changing Times

Beginning in the 1600s, the Inuit began trading furs and hides with the Hudson's Bay Company for tools and food, and their lives gradually began to change. But the biggest changes occurred in the 1930s when the fur market collapsed. In 1941, the government made the Inuit wards of the state. In the 1950s, many Inuit were relocated from their villages. Children were taken from their parents and placed in residential schools.

Inuit Land Claims

In 1976, the Inuit presented their first land claims to the government and voiced their desire to establish a new territory with Inuktitut as its official language. In 1982, a clause protecting Aboriginal land claims was added to the Canadian constitution. It was a long journey but the actual birth date of the new territory on April 1, 1999, was a cause for celebration and became an international news story.

WOULD YOU BELIEVE . . . ?
Nunavut covers a vast territory — one-fifth of Canada's land mass.

HE WAS YOUNG AND COURAGEOUS, AND HE WAS ON A MISSION. WITH EVERY STEP TERRY FOX TOOK IN HIS HEROIC RUN, HE RAISED HOPE FOR CANCER PATIENTS EVERYWHERE.

A Start in Newfoundland

Terry Fox lost his leg to cancer when he was only 18 years old. It could have slowed him down but instead it galvanized him into action. After an intense training period, Fox started his Marathon of Hope in St. John's, Newfoundland. On April 12, 1980, he dipped his artificial leg in the Atlantic Ocean and filled two large water bottles. He planned to keep one as a souvenir and pour the other into the Pacific Ocean when he completed his run.

Marathon Days

The first days were difficult. Gale-force winds, heavy rain and a snowstorm pelted Fox. At first his efforts didn't attract much attention but gradually his spirit and perseverance made him a national hero. It seemed nothing could stop this young man, not even pain.

But in late August, when cancer spread to his lung, Fox was forced to end his run in Thunder Bay, Ontario. He'd been running for 143 days and had covered 5,373 kilometres. He returned home for treatment but the following year the nation mourned when he died on June 28, 1981.

The Hope Continues

Though Fox was gone, the impact of what he'd achieved was only beginning. Terry Fox Runs, still held annually, have raised more than $650 million for cancer research worldwide.

> **WOULD YOU BELIEVE . . . ?**
> On average Fox ran a marathon distance (42 kilometres) every day, seven days a week.

"I believe in miracles. I have to."
— Terry Fox

VANCOUVER 2010
Celebrating sport Vancouver style

EACH OLYMPICS REFLECTS THE ATHLETES, THE TIMES, THE WEATHER AND THE LOCATION. THE 2010 VANCOUVER OLYMPICS WAS NO EXCEPTION.

Facts and Highlights

- The longest Olympic torch relay ever; it took 106 days to carry the torch across Canada.
- 82 nations and 2,566 athletes participated.
- Canada was the first host country since Norway in 1952 to win the most gold medals. Canada broke the record, with 14 gold!
- The most accessible Olympics for people with disabilities and the first to use environmentally friendly criteria for new construction.
- For the first time, Aboriginal peoples were recognized as official Olympic participants and were involved in all aspects of the games.

After the Olympics

The Vancouver Olympics cost more than $7 billion but it led to many upgrades in the city such as the Sea-to-Sky Highway improvement, the Canada Line rapid transit to the Vancouver Airport and the Vancouver Convention Centre.

WOULD YOU BELIEVE . . . ?
The Royal Canadian Mint made more than 1,000 medals for the 2010 Olympic and Paralympic Games. Each medal is unique, reflecting the individual athlete it was awarded to.

Canada has hosted the Olympics twice before: in 1976, Montreal welcomed the summer games and in 1988, Calgary hosted the winter Olympics.

People who call Canada home have rocketed into space, zoomed over our dense forests and gazed up into our glittering night skies. Some people in our country have even dreamed of visitors who come from planets far, far away. Get ready to take flight with ten uplifting Canadian stories.

CHAPTER 4

HIGH-FLYING CANADA

Ideas and Inventions that Make Us Soar

FRANKS' G-SUIT
Fighting gravity to win the war

AT THE BEGINNING OF WORLD WAR II, FIGHTER PILOTS FACED THE THREAT OF SUDDEN BLACKOUTS WHEN THEIR PLANES ACCELERATED QUICKLY. WILBUR R. FRANKS WANTED TO HELP THESE BRAVE FLYERS.

An Anti-Gravity Solution

High-speed manoeuvres in fighter planes made it tough for a pilot's heart to pump blood to his brain. The pilot often lost consciousness, which could have deadly consequences.

In 1941, Franks, a Canadian doctor and inventor, came up with a water-filled anti-gravity suit called a G-suit. This close-fitting rubber suit had two layers. The inner one lay against the pilot's skin, while the outer layer was filled with water. The liquid pressed on the pilot's legs and stomach, keeping his blood circulating normally, instead of pooling in the lower parts of his body. The concept behind the Franks Flying Suit is also the basis of the suits today's air force pilots and astronauts wear.

Gee, That Makes Sense!

To test the G-suit and further help pilots, Franks also invented the Human Centrifuge. This machine whirled pilots around to simulate the gravitational forces (known as G forces) pilots experience at high speeds. That gave pilots training for combat. Franks' work gave Canadian pilots, and their allies, an advantage over enemy pilots and helped the Canadian (Allied) side win World War II.

> ### WOULD YOU BELIEVE . . . ?
> Franks' inventions saved thousands of lives — it's estimated at least five times more pilots survived World War II than would have without the G-suit.

LONG-DISTANCE FLIERS
Great migrations

SOME CANADIAN FLIERS *ARE WORLD-RECORD HOLDERS. THEY TRAVEL ASTONISHING DISTANCES BY AIR.*

No Terning Back

Each year, the Arctic tern, a medium-sized white seabird, flies all the way from its home on Canada's Arctic tundra to the ocean off Antarctica. Then a few months later, it flies all the way back. That's a round trip of more than 70,000 kilometres each year — the record for the world's longest migration.

Are we there yet?

This strong flier can live more than 30 years. So throughout its life, it may fly more than 2.1 million kilometres, or to the moon and back three times.

Flying Royalty

Canada's monarch butterfly wins the prize for the insect that migrates the farthest. They can fly up to 4,500 kilometres to their wintering ground. For years, scientists had no idea where that was. Canadians Fred and Norah Urquhart spent 38 years searching for the site in Mexico and in 1975 they finally discovered it.

WOULD YOU BELIEVE . . . ?

Arctic terns live in large colonies, yet somehow they all know when it's time to begin migrating. Just before they fly away, the noisy colony suddenly becomes quiet, then they all take to the air.

Scientists are still trying to figure out how the new generation in the spring knows how to return to the places their parents and grandparents spent their summer. Some experts think the butterflies use Earth's magnetic field; others think the monarchs orient themselves to the sun.

CHAMPION MIGRATORS

Arctic tern	35,000 kilometres
Humpback whale	8,500 kilometres
Monarch butterfly	4,500 kilometres
Caribou	1,125 kilometres

CANADARM IS A GIANT ROBOTIC ARM THAT MADE A NAME FOR CANADA IN SPACE. THANKS TO THIS AMAZING TOOL, CANADA IS RECOGNIZED AS A LEADER IN THE ROBOTICS FIELD.

Canadarm

First used on the space shuttle *Columbia* in 1981, Canadarm had joints that work like your shoulder, elbow and wrist.

The robotic arm made life much safer and easier for astronauts. On a space shuttle *Discovery* mission in 1984, ice had built up on a shuttle vent. That could have been a dangerous problem, but one tap with Canadarm and the ice broke off and floated away. Canadarm maintained the various space shuttles while they were in orbit, was used to repair the Hubble Space Telescope and helped construct the International Space Station (ISS).

Canadarm2

Canadarm was retired after 90 shuttle missions but Canadarm2 continues to help astronauts on the ISS. It is slightly longer than the first model, about four times heavier, and it's more flexible — its joints can rotate more than your arm joints can.

Lending a Hand

Dextre is another Canadian robot used by astronauts on the ISS. Equipped with tools and a camera, Dextre, also known as Canada Hand, can be fastened to the end of Canadarm2 and positioned at different work sites.

In February 2011, for its first official task, Dextre unpacked equipment while the crew on the ISS slept.

CHRIS HADFIELD
Commander Canada

USING TWEETS, PHOTOS, VIDEOS AND SONGS, CHRIS HADFIELD ENGAGED THE WORLD WITH SPACE TRAVEL LIKE NEVER BEFORE.

Realizing a Dream

When Hadfield was a boy, he dreamed of being an astronaut. First he became a fighter pilot. In June 1992, he was one of four astronauts chosen by the Canadian Space Program from more than 5,000 applicants. Three years later he became the first Canadian to board a Russian spacecraft and to use the Canadarm.

A Fleet of Firsts

Hadfield has had many firsts in his career. On his initial trip to the ISS in 2001, he became the first Canadian to leave a spacecraft and float freely in space. In December 2012, Hadfield began a five-month-long stay on the ISS. He was the commander, the first Canadian to hold this top position. He also made the first-ever music video shot in space, with his rendition of David Bowie's hit song "Space Oddity."

Bringing Space within Reach

Hadfield greatly increased general understanding of space by answering questions people sent him, including: does your nose run more in space (it can't because there's no gravity); what happens when you sneeze while wearing your helmet (it's messy); and do you burp in space (no).

WOULD YOU BELIEVE . . . ?

Chris Hadfield is scared of heights! Peering over the edge of a tall building makes his stomach feel queasy. But, he says, astronauts have to be prepared to deal with many things, some of them very dangerous.

NORTHERN CANADA IS FULL OF REMOTE SETTLEMENTS THAT DEPEND ON PLANES TO BRING IN SUPPLIES. IT TAKES A SPECIAL AIRCRAFT TO BRAVE THE HARSH CONDITIONS.

Only in a Bush Plane . . .

You can't mistake a bush plane for anything else. It's designed to be fitted with floats so it can land on water, skis for snow landings, and wheels for landing on ground. Those tires may be very large so the

plane can safely take off from broken ground — sometimes runways in the North are very short or don't exist at all!

The high wings on a bush plane make it easy to load and unload, especially from docks. That wing position also reduces the possibility of damage during a rough landing or takeoff. Bush planes also have a small rear wheel. While other types of planes have a nose wheel, that can be harder to repair than a tail wheel, and a damaged front wheel can prevent an aircraft from flying.

The Norseman earned the nicknames "the workhorse of the skies" and "the one-ton flying truck" because it was rugged, reliable and had a large cargo area.

Flying *Norseman*

These tough little aircraft that opened up Canada's northern wilderness also saw military action. One of the most popular was the *Norseman*, the first Canadian-designed bush plane. Built in 1935 by Montrealer Robert Noorduyn, it was flown by Canadian and American pilots in World War II.

A NORTHERN LIGHT SHOW
Those dazzling skies!

NORTHERN CANADA IS ONE OF THE BEST PLACES IN THE WORLD TO SEE THIS AMAZING LIGHT SHOW, ALSO KNOWN AS AURORA BOREALIS.

What's the Glow?

The northern lights' rippling curtains of colour are produced when gas particles in Earth's atmosphere collide with electrically charged particles from the sun's atmosphere. The sun throws off those particles as it rotates, and they're blown toward Earth on the solar wind. Most of the particles are deflected by the magnetic field that surrounds Earth. But the field is weaker at the poles, so some particles enter there.

Look *and* Listen

The best times of year to see the northern lights are around March 21 and September 21. That's when the magnetic fields of Earth and the sun are most closely lined up.

If the sun's charged particles bump oxygen molecules high in the atmosphere, the gas molecules shine red. If the sun's electric particles hit oxygen molecules closer to Earth, they glow green. When nitrogen particles are struck, they shine violet.

And don't forget to listen, too. Some people claim they hear claps and hissing sounds when they watch the northern lights. Scientists say these are caused by solar particles high above the ground.

WOULD YOU BELIEVE . . . ?

Canada has more Dark-Sky Preserves (DSPs) than all other countries combined. DSPs are areas free of light pollution, making it easier to see stars and other night sky phenomena. The largest DSP in the world is Wood Buffalo National Park, in the Northwest Territories and Alberta.

CANADIAN BROADCASTING CORPORATION
Cross-Canada communications

CANADA BUILT ITS FIRST RADIO STATIONS IN 1922, IN CITIES SUCH AS MONTREAL, VANCOUVER AND EDMONTON. IT SOON BECAME CLEAR THE COUNTRY NEEDED A NATIONAL BROADCASTER TO SERVE CANADIANS.

A National Broadcaster

In the early days of radio, many American radio stations were broadcasting into Canada. The Canadian government wanted to protect and reflect Canadian culture with broadcasting of our own. In 1936, the Canadian Broadcasting Corporation (CBC) was born, along with the French network known as Radio-Canada.

WOULD YOU BELIEVE . . . ?
Today, the network is also available on the Web and not only broadcasts radio in French and English but in eight Aboriginal languages as well.

Back then, 10 hours of French and English programs were offered daily. About 10 years later, this had increased to a total of 43 hours each day in both languages. To appeal to all Canadians, broadcasts included hockey games, royal visits, shows for farmers and more.

And Then Came Television

In 1952 the first CBC and Radio-Canada (which became known as Ici Radio-Canada Télé) television stations began broadcasting from Toronto and Montreal. Uncle Chichimus, a bald puppet, and his niece Hollyhock (below) appeared on the first broadcast. By 1955, television was available to 66% of Canadians.

Three years later, the country saw its first coast-to-coast live television broadcast. Canadian television took another big step forward in 1973 with the first live television service to the North, thanks to the Anik A1 satellite.

TELESAT CANADA LAUNCHED THE ANIK SATELLITE ON NOVEMBER 9, 1972. CANADA BECAME THE FIRST COUNTRY TO HAVE ITS OWN NATIONAL COMMUNICATIONS SATELLITE.

Calling All Canadians

The Anik satellite improved telephone communication and television transmission across the whole nation. It was built with a signal beam that covered from Canada's Atlantic coast to its Pacific shores and from the American border to above the Arctic Circle. By 1976, Canada had launched two more Anik satellites so there would be backup in case of any satellite failures and users would have continuous service.

The Anik satellites had a wide tube, or cylinder, for a body. The cylinder spun, which kept the satellite stable. The antenna looked like a broad, shallow bowl and was always directed toward Canada. Solar cells on the tube provided power.

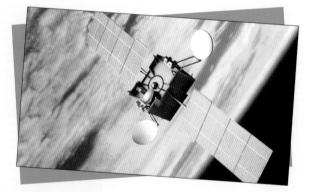

Meet the Anik Family

The satellite that was launched in 1972 became known as Anik A1 because it was just the first of many Anik satellites. Anik A1 was retired in 1982. When Anik F1 was launched on November 21, 2000, it was the most powerful communications satellite ever built. At least five Anik satellites are still in use, while more than ten have been retired.

Telesat Canada held a naming contest when the satellite launched. Anik was chosen because it means "little brother" in Inuktitut, and symbolized bringing Canadians together in a national brotherhood.

UNIDENTIFIED FLYING OBJECTS
Extraterrestrials welcome here

CANADA IS HOME TO THE WORLD'S FIRST, AND SO FAR ONLY, UFO LANDING PAD. SINCE 1967, THE TOWN OF ST. PAUL, ALBERTA, HAS PROVIDED A PLACE FOR EXTRATERRESTRIAL VISITORS TO TOUCH DOWN ON EARTH.

Take Me to Your Leader

St. Paul, located near the border with Saskatchewan, has an information centre that includes exhibits on UFOs, as well as a hotline to call in UFO sightings. Thanks to its unusual landmark, St. Paul has hosted UFO conferences that people come from around the world to attend. The landing pad has even had a regal visitor: Queen Elizabeth II stopped by in 1978.

Still Waiting . . .

The UFO pad was built in 1967 to mark Canada's centennial year. At the time, people were excited about space travel — just two years later, astronauts would walk on the moon. It seemed a fitting way to celebrate the nation and look forward to its next 100 years. So far, it doesn't seem as if any alien spacecraft have landed here. But if one comes whirring by, Canada is ready.

Free Parking

The sign beside the UFO landing pad reads: "The area under the world's first UFO landing pad was designated international by the town of St. Paul as a symbol of our faith that mankind will maintain the outer universe free from national wars and strife. That future travel in space will be safe for all intergalactic beings, all visitors from Earth or otherwise are welcome to this territory and to the town of St. Paul."

NELVANA OF THE NORTHERN LIGHTS

A Truly Canadian superhero

SHE COULD READ MINDS, TRAVEL AT LIGHTSPEED ALONG A RAY OF NORTHERN LIGHTS AND KEEP CANADA SAFE DURING WORLD WAR II.

Crime Fighter Extraordinaire

During World War II, the Canadian government banned luxury goods made in the United States. This was to help our economy but, to the horror of many kids, the ban included comic books. Canadian publishers stepped in and created hundreds of original Canadian comic book characters to fill the gap.

Nelvana of the Northern Lights was one of the most popular. North America's first female superhero, Nelvana fought evil and Nazi spies in comic books from 1941 until 1947.

Nelvana's creator, Adrian Dingle, was inspired by Inuit tales when he created her stories.

A Hero for Difficult Times

Fighting crime in Canada's North, Nelvana could become invisible and had super breath. Thanks to the power of the northern lights, she could disrupt electronic signals and shoot out energy blasts. Nelvana was aided by her father, an Inuk God named Koliak the Mighty, and her brother, Tanero. During the dark days of World War II, when it sometimes seemed as if the enemy Axis forces were going to win, Nelvana raised Canadians' spirits.

WOULD YOU BELIEVE . . . ?

The first of the great comic book superheroes, Superman, was also created by a Canadian. Joe Shuster began drawing the Man of Steel when he was just 17 years old. Superman's secret identity was Clark Kent, a character Shuster modelled on himself. Superman's home city of Metropolis was based on Toronto, Shuster's original hometown.

What's in a name?
A lot! Discover why,
and how, strange and
interesting names such
as Kicking Horse Pass,
Head-Smashed-In Buffalo
Jump, hoodoo and Mount
Royal came to be. There's
a story behind each one.

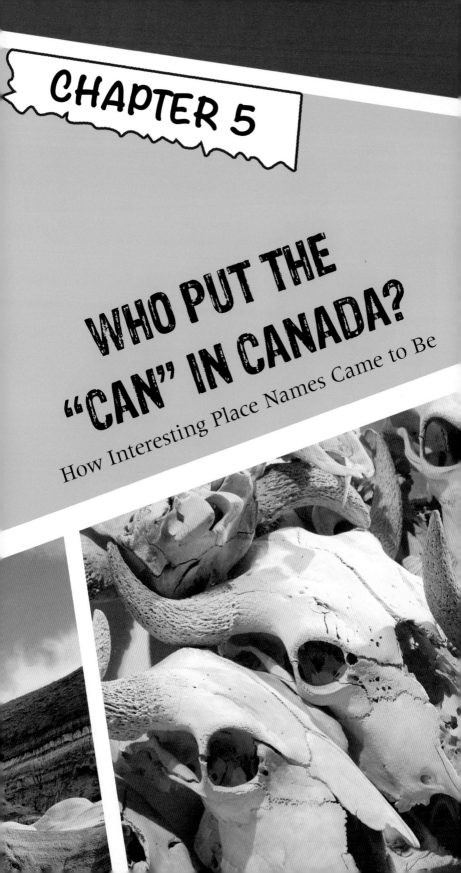

CHAPTER 5

WHO PUT THE "CAN" IN CANADA?

How Interesting Place Names Came to Be

THE ROCKY MOUNTAINS
How rocky are they?

THE ROCKIES ARE MAJESTIC, MAGNIFICENT AND, YOU GUESSED IT, ROCKY. THIS RUGGED MOUNTAIN RANGE DRAWS CLIMBERS, HIKERS AND NATURE LOVERS, NOT TO MENTION THE WILDLIFE THAT CALL IT HOME.

Rock on!

Us vs. U.S.

The Canadian Rockies run from the north end of British Columbia to the U.S. border, between Alberta and B.C. The range continues south through the U.S. Here are four ways that the Canadian and American Rockies differ:

There are five spectacular national parks in the Canadian Rockies: Banff, Jasper, Kootenay, Yoho and Waterton Lakes. All are designated UNESCO Heritage sites.

1. The Canadian Rockies are sharper and pointier with wide valleys, thanks to the glaciers that formed them. The U.S. Rockies are more rounded.

2. The Canadian Rockies are cooler and wetter, with moister soil.

3. Most of the Canadian Rockies are made of the sedimentary (layered and compacted) rocks shale and limestone. Most of the U.S. Rockies are igneous (formed when molten materials like lava cool and solidify) and metamorphic (rocks changed by heat or pressure from one form into another without passing through a liquid stage).

4. The treeline is lower in the Canadian Rockies.

KICKING HORSE PASS
Who kicked whom?

WHAT DOES A KICKING HORSE HAVE TO DO WITH BUILDING THE CANADIAN PACIFIC RAILWAY?

A Promise

It started with a promise: prime minister John A. Macdonald vowed to build a railway connecting B.C. to the rest of Canada by 1881, 10 years after B.C. joined Confederation. What stood in the way? Mountains!

Macdonald hired engineer Walter Moberly to find the best route. He chose one that snaked through the mountains via Kicking Horse Pass. It would pass through prairie land, shorten the western section of the route and bring transportation and trade closer to the United States. It would bypass the rugged Rockies but run smack into the almost impassable Selkirk Mountains.

But Why Is It Called Kicking Horse Pass?

While trying to find a pass through the Selkirk Mountains, surgeon Dr. James Hector, who was part of the 1857–60 Palliser Expedition, was kicked by his horse. The name stuck.

So, the horse just kicked you?

Yes.

WOULD YOU BELIEVE . . . ?

The steep and dangerous Kicking Horse Pass caused so many accidents that in 1909 the CPR built an alternative route called the Spiral Tunnels. Now the railway could haul dining and sleeping cars through the mountain more easily.

HEAD-SMASHED-IN BUFFALO JUMP
One, two, three, over

THIS FAMOUS SITE IS WEST OF FORT MACLEOD, ALBERTA, WHERE THE FOOTHILLS OF THE ROCKIES MEET THE GREAT PLAINS.

The Buffalo Hunt

About 5,000 years ago Aboriginal peoples hunted buffalo for food, clothing and shelter without any weapons — not even bows and arrows. Instead they drove the buffalo herds over the cliffs of the site we now call Head-Smashed-In Buffalo Jump.

Before the hunt, a ceremony was held where everyone prayed for success. Then buffalo runners, disguised under animal hides, fanned out to locate the herd, gather them together and lure them toward the cliffs. Some hunters used V-shaped lanes lined with stone cairns to direct the animals toward the cliffs. Others hid behind brush, shouting and waving buffalo hides to keep the buffalo going. And when the buffalo neared the edge of the cliff, the hunters rushed out and drove the animals over. After the hunt, every part of the buffalo was used — for meat, tools and shelter.

Why the Name?

Legend has it that a young Blackfoot warrior was hiding under the cliff, sheltered by a ledge. He got trapped as the buffalo went over. You can imagine the rest . . .

WOULD YOU BELIEVE . . . ?

The buffalo jump site was abandoned for 1,000 years. No one knows why, but it resumed about 1,800 years ago. Most of the artifacts we've found are from that last period. The jump ended again once guns and horses came on the scene and changed the hunt.

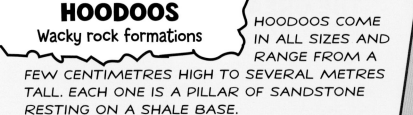

HOODOOS COME IN ALL SIZES AND RANGE FROM A FEW CENTIMETRES HIGH TO SEVERAL METRES TALL. EACH ONE IS A PILLAR OF SANDSTONE RESTING ON A SHALE BASE.

What's a Hoodoo Do?

Hoodoos are rocks sculpted by frost, rain, wind, erosion and time. The word *hoodoo* probably comes from *voodoo*, a West African-based religion centred on magic. And there is certainly a magical feel to these oddly shaped rocks that look like they come from an alien planet.

Hoodoos take millions of years to develop into their out-of-this-world shapes.

How to Find a Hoodoo

Hoodoos dot the Canadian Badlands in Alberta and attract thousands of visitors intrigued by their strange, often mushroom-like shapes. You can visit hoodoos in Dinosaur Provincial Park and Writing-on-Stone Provincial Park, on the Milk River. But don't jump on a hoodoo. They're fragile.

Hoodoo Art

Writing-on-Stone Provincial Park is not only full of hoodoos but is also one of the most important spiritual sites for the Blackfoot people. The park has many hoodoos with images etched into the rock. The rock carvings, called petroglyphs, were often created using antlers or bones. The rock paintings, called pictographs, were made using crushed iron ore mixed with water, or a piece of ironstone. Some of the hoodoo images are thousands of years old; some were carved less than 300 years ago.

THE GREAT LAKES
What's so great about them?

THERE ARE FIVE GREAT LAKES.

THEY ARE MAJOR TRANSPORTATION ROUTES AND COMPRISE THE LARGEST GROUP OF FRESHWATER LAKES IN THE WORLD.

In the Beginning

Around 10,000 years ago, during the last glacial period, retreating ice sheets created the Great Lakes. Aboriginal peoples were the first to settle around them, followed by Europeans in the 1700s. The area around the lakes was good for farming and the lakes themselves provided transportation routes for trade.

Today the area around Lakes Erie and Ontario continues to be heavily populated. The western end of Lake Ontario is called the Golden Horseshoe because of its dense population and industry.

The Great Lakes contain 21% of the world's surface freshwater.

Lake Superior — I'm the biggest!

Lake Huron — I have the most shoreline, counting my islands.

Lake Michigan — I'm all-American.

Lake Ontario — I'm the smallest.

Lake Erie — I'm the shallowest.

WOULD YOU BELIEVE . . . ?

Over the last century chemicals seeping in from nearby farms have damaged the Great Lakes. Sea creatures such as zebra mussels, sea lampreys and ruffe that have arrived clinging to the hulls of tankers or ships, or slipped in through the Welland Canal, have also invaded the lakes. These species have affected fish colonies and increased toxic algae.

THE THOUSAND ISLANDS
Keep on counting . . .

WE CALL THEM THE THOUSAND ISLANDS, BUT THERE REALLY ARE MORE LIKE 1,865 ISLANDS, BETWEEN CANADA AND THE UNITED STATES.

Why So Many Little Islands?

Glaciers and floods thousands of years ago turned hilltops into islands in Lake Ontario and the St. Lawrence. Plants and animals migrated to the islands, attracted by the mild climate and rugged, rocky landscape. The islands come in all sizes and shapes and are made mostly of granite. Some belong to Canada and some to the U.S.

Getting Around

There are so many rocks and shoals (shallow, sandy spots) around the Thousand Islands that you not only need a boat but also experience to navigate them. It used to be difficult to see through the murky water but since zebra mussels arrived (mostly a nuisance but in this case a help) they've eaten the algae and cleared the water. You can also drive from Canada to the U.S. (or vice versa) via the Thousand Islands Bridge.

UNESCO notes the Thousand Islands-Frontenac Arch region as a World Biosphere Reserve. Around 20 islands make up Thousand Islands National Park in Canada.

HOW TO QUALIFY?

To be one of the thousand islands, you have to:

1. Be above ground all year round.

2. Cover an area bigger than 0.093 square metres.

3. Have at least one growing tree.

TROIS-RIVIÈRES
Demand a recount!

HALFWAY BETWEEN MONTREAL AND QUEBEC LIES A CITY CALLED TROIS-RIVIÈRES, WHICH MEANS THREE RIVERS.

Un, deux . . . quoi?

How Many Rivers Meet There?

In fact only two. The "three" refers to three mouths, or channels, of the Saint-Maurice River.

> "This small settlement had become the meeting ground of the hardy spirits who had an itching of the foot, the coureurs de bois. Quebec was the port . . . Trois-Rivières was the starting point of exploration."
> — Author Thomas Costain

Who Settled Here?

For centuries the Algonquin and Abernaki people lived in the area during the summer. The French explorer Jacques Cartier landed there in 1536 and another explorer, Captain Dupont, dubbed it Trois-Rivières in 1599.

In 1634, a colony was established, the second colony in New France after Quebec. The colony became a thriving centre of trade and government. In 1776 Americans mounted an unsuccessful invasion in the Battle of Trois-Rivières.

Burned Down and Rebuilt

In 1908 a young boy struck a match in a dark shed while hunting for his lost ball, and a strong dry wind fuelled a raging fire. Much of the present city was rebuilt after that devastating fire.

MOUNT ROYAL
The city's heart and playground

THERE'S A BEAUTIFUL BIG HILL IN THE CITY OF MONTREAL CALLED MOUNT ROYAL. IT'S AS REGAL AS A MOUNTAIN BUT NOT HIGH ENOUGH TO BE DESIGNATED ONE.

A High Point

Explorer Jacques Cartier, the first European to climb it, named the peak in 1535.

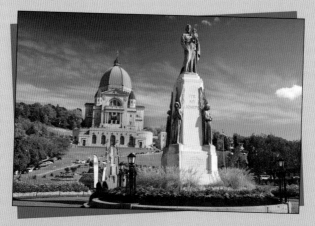

A Gathering Place

In the 1860s there was a huge public outcry when people started cutting down trees on Mount Royal for firewood. The city of Montreal hired the great landscape designer of New York's Central Park, Frederick Law Olmsted, to landscape part of Mount Royal and turn it into an urban park. Although many of Olmsted's suggestions were never executed because Montreal suffered a depression in the mid-1870s, a park was created.

In 1998, a lot of the old trees in the park were damaged in an ice storm. Many have since recovered, and in 2000 the government of Quebec and Montreal jointly gave the park permanent protection and established its unique place in the life of the city.

WOULD YOU BELIEVE . . . ?

In 1992, a time capsule was placed on Mount Royal in honour of Montreal's 350th anniversary. The capsule, which has messages and drawings from children noting their visions for the city, will be opened in 2142.

THE FLOWERPOT ROCKS
Sculpted by water, ice and time

THE FAMOUS HOPEWELL ROCKS IN NEW BRUNSWICK'S BAY OF FUNDY ARE ALSO KNOWN AS THE FLOWERPOT ROCKS.

How Were the Pots Created?

Millions of years ago, mountains stood in this area. Over time the mountains eroded as mud, pebbles and rocks washed into the valleys. Eventually, the loose rocks compressed into solid rocks and, after the ice age, formed the Bay of Fundy. Ice and rain and the tides continue to shape the rocks into the strange and wonderful formations you see today. Visitors love to explore the giant rocks at low tide on foot and in high tide by kayak.

Legends and Tales

The local Mi'kmaq people who've lived in the area for centuries have passed on stories of how these unusual rock shapes came to be. In one tale some poor Mi'kmaq were held captive by angry whales in the bay. When they tried to escape, the whales turned them into stone.

Always Changing

Not all the rocks look like flowerpots either. Some look like people or creatures and some are nicknamed just that. There's the ET Rock, the Dinosaur Rock and the Mother-in-Law Rock. And the shapes will keep changing. The continued erosion will keep whittling away, and creating and reshaping them.

THE ROCK
Talk about a rocky province!

NEWFOUNDLAND IS A BIG, ROCK-FILLED ISLAND. IT'S THE SIXTEENTH-LARGEST ISLAND IN THE WORLD AND CANADA'S FOURTH-LARGEST ISLAND.

Who Landed on the Rock?

As the closest place in North America to Europe, it's not surprising that Norse Vikings, led by the intrepid Leif Erickson, landed here. In 1962, clear evidence of a Viking settlement was discovered in L'Anse aux Meadows on the northern tip of Newfoundland.

The Vikings probably had contact with the local Beothuk people, who inhabited the area. In 1497, explorer Jacques Cartier sailed here, and in 1583 Sir Humphrey Gilbert claimed Newfoundland as England's first colony in North America. Many more Europeans arrived in the eighteenth and nineteenth centuries, attracted by the abundance of cod and other fish. Unfortunately, due to overfishing, the cod industry fell apart in the second half the 20th century.

Newfoundland rocks are some of the oldest and most unusual anywhere. Geologists come from all over to study them.

WOULD YOU BELIEVE . . . ?
Many Newfoundland towns have colourful and unique names such as Heart's Content, Come By Chance, Witless Bay and Main Tickle. There's also "Mistaken Point Ecological Reserve," which isn't a mistake but a spot to find fossils of some of the oldest creatures found anywhere on Earth, dating back 565 million years.

Sports, medicine, entertainment, even the way the world tells time: Canada has been changing them all for hundreds of years. Here are ten of the top ways Canadians have made the world a better place.

CHAPTER 6

CANADA DID IT!

Transforming People, Places and Ideas

THE SCIENTISTS WHO STILL HELP MILLIONS
A medical miracle

FOR HUNDREDS OF YEARS, DIABETES WAS A DEATH SENTENCE. THIS ILLNESS MADE IT SO DIFFICULT FOR PEOPLE TO DIGEST IMPORTANT NUTRIENTS THAT THEY USUALLY DIED.

How to Keep a Disease in Check

Frederick Banting lost a friend to diabetes when he was just a teen. No wonder that when Banting became a doctor, working at the University of Toronto, he decided to study the disease. Working with diabetic dogs, Banting (right) and researchers Charles Best (left) and James Collip discovered the hormone insulin in 1921. It kept the dogs alive — but what about humans? The first diabetic person given insulin was a 14-year-old boy, in 1922, and it worked!

A Second Chance at Life

In the early 1920s, children with diabetes were kept in hospitals, as many as 50 to a room, most so ill they were in comas. Imagine how their families felt watching Banting, Best and Collip going from bed to bed, injecting the dying children with insulin.

Before the scientists reached the last child, the first ones were waking from their comas. It must have seemed like a miracle. Insulin isn't a cure for diabetes, but it helps control the disease, and it continues to save the lives of millions of people around the world.

Which of these medical discoveries and inventions are Canadian?
A. Artificial human heart
B. Discovery of gene for cystic fibrosis (a disease affecting the lungs and other organs)
C. Portable, fast blood test (even used by astronauts in space)
D. Heart pacemaker (keeps heart beating regularly)

Answer: They are all Canadian!

A WORLDWIDE SYSTEM OF TIME
Not a minute too soon!

AN UNCOMFORTABLE NIGHT IN A RAILWAY STATION LED TO A WORLD-CHANGING INVENTION. SANDFORD FLEMING'S SLEEPLESS NIGHT DUE TO A CONFUSING TRAIN SCHEDULE CAUSED HIM TO CHANGE HOW THE WORLD TELLS TIME.

Trying to Track Time

By the mid-1800s, North America had 144 official time zones! Each community had its own time, based on the sun, and the zones advanced by one minute for every 18 kilometres to the east. It was almost impossible to keep track of them all.

It wasn't a big problem when 18 kilometres was considered a long trip. But when the railway was built across the country and passengers began moving faster and farther, watch out! Many passengers began carrying more than one watch. Not only did people miss connections, but sometimes trains found themselves on the same track, speeding toward each other — yikes!

Better Late than Never

In 1879, Fleming proposed a worldwide system of 24 time zones, each an hour different from the next. At first the idea was totally rejected. But Fleming worked hard to convince scientists and businessmen. Standard Time came into use around the world on January 1, 1885. Today Canada has six time zones.

> ### WOULD YOU BELIEVE . . . ?
> Fleming not only supervised the building of Canada's cross-country railway in the early 1880s, he also designed Canada's first postage stamp. Issued in 1851, the stamp known as the Threepenny Beaver can be worth hundreds of dollars today!

VIOLA DESMOND'S REFUSAL
Standing up to discrimination

ON NOVEMBER 8, 1946, VIOLA DESMOND, A BLACK HAIRDRESSER AND BUSINESSWOMAN, WAS DRIVING TO A MEETING WHEN HER CAR BROKE DOWN IN NEW GLASGOW, NOVA SCOTIA. LITTLE DID SHE KNOW THAT DAY WOULD GO DOWN IN HISTORY.

When Enough Is Enough

When Desmond discovered she'd be stuck overnight for car repairs, she bought a movie ticket and took a seat on the theatre's main floor. The manager quickly tried to force Desmond to move. She didn't realize she'd been sold a ticket for the balcony. Desmond attempted to buy a ticket for the main floor, but the staff wouldn't sell her one — only white people could sit in the better part of the theatre. So Desmond refused to move. She'd finally had enough of racial discrimination.

A Slow Pardon

A policeman had to carry Desmond out and she spent the night in jail, charged with attempting to cheat the Province of Nova Scotia. That's because tax on the balcony-seat ticket she'd been sold was one cent less than on the main-floor seat. No one mentioned skin colour — but everyone knew that's what the arrest was all about.

The case became one of the most publicized incidents of racial discrimination in Canada. Desmond died in 1965, but in 2010, she finally received an apology for her wrongful arrest. In 2012, Canada Post issued a stamp honouring Desmond.

"What happened to my sister is part of our history ... We must learn from our history so we do not repeat it. If my parents were here today, it would warm their hearts to see Viola recognized as a true Canadian hero."
— Wanda Robson, Viola Desmond's sister,
April 15, 2010

ROBERTSON SCREWDRIVER
A new twist

PETER L. ROBERTSON WAS DEMONSTRATING A SCREWDRIVER AT A TRADE SHOW WHEN THE TOOL SUDDENLY SLIPPED AND CUT HIS HAND. LUCKILY, ROBERTSON WASN'T ONLY A SALESMAN; HE WAS ALSO AN INVENTOR. HE WENT ON TO CHANGE CONSTRUCTION HISTORY.

Safety Squared

Robertson knew many workers hurt themselves using screwdrivers. He decided to create one that wouldn't slip in action. Robertson invented a screw with a square-shaped socket on its head,

and a screwdriver with a matching square on its end that fit snugly into the screw head.

WOULD YOU BELIEVE . . . ?

Here's another world-changing Canadian invention: in 1930 John D. Millar came up with the idea of painting lines on the road to make car travel safer. By 1933, this innovation spread from Ontario and Quebec to all across North America.

And Speedy, Too!

The Robertson screwdriver was a hit around the world and it still is. Both the tool and the socket on the screw head have a taper, which makes the tool simpler to insert. Also, the taper helps keep the screw on the tip of the screwdriver so the user doesn't have to hold it there. That means the Robertson screwdriver can be used with one hand. Robertson's invention sped up work and reduced frustration.

Canadian Norman Breakey sped up the task of painting by inventing the paint roller in 1940.

NAISMITH'S GAME
Follow the bouncing ball

CANADIANS AND AMERICANS BOTH LIKE TO CLAIM THIS ONE, BUT THE POPULAR SPORT OF BASKETBALL WAS INVENTED BY A CANADIAN WHO WAS LIVING IN THE UNITED STATES.

Shooting Hoops

In December 1891, Canadian James Naismith was an instructor at a college in Springfield, Massachusetts. He had to invent an indoor winter sport for the students that was energetic but not too rough. Naismith tried indoor football, lacrosse and soccer but none of them worked well. Then Naismith had the idea of using a large ball that players had to toss into peach baskets nailed up at either end of the gym.

Naismith wrote up rules, including penalties for rough play, and stipulated that players couldn't run with the ball but had to pass it. The game was a hit but there was one big problem: every time the ball went in the basket, the janitor had to climb up and get it down. Soon someone had the good idea of cutting the bottoms out of the baskets.

WOULD YOU BELIEVE . . . ?

Synchronized swimming was also invented by a Canadian, Peg Seller, in the 1920s. And five-pin bowling was first played in 1909 in Toronto. Thomas F. Ryan, a bowling alley owner, created it when people complained about how heavy the balls and pins were in the original ten-pin game.

Pass the Boxball!

Some students wanted to call the new sport Naismithball. Naismith preferred the name basketball. Originally he'd asked for boxes, not baskets, for his game. Imagine — today millions could be playing "boxball" instead!

Steve Nash was named the National Basketball Association's Most Valuable Player in 2005 *and* 2006. He's the only Canadian to ever earn this honour.

THE ANIMAL THAT CHANGED HISTORY
Do you like my hat?

THE BEAVER HAS HAD A BIGGER IMPACT ON CANADIAN HISTORY AND EXPLORATION THAN ANY OTHER ANIMAL OR PLANT. NO WONDER IT HAS BECOME A SYMBOL OF OUR COUNTRY.

MVP (Most Valuable Pelt)

European countries would not likely have explored and fought over Canada if it weren't for the beaver. Beaver pelts were the most valuable furs in the 1600s, and the best ones came from Canada. They were turned into beaver hats, which were were status symbols for Europeans at the time.

It's not easy being an icon.

And Waterproof, Too!

The beaver is built to be under water. Even when a beaver has been submerged for six or seven minutes, it's still not wet to the skin. It secretes a waterproof oil that it spreads through its thick hair.

Beavers build dams and lodges, making them one of the only mammals, besides humans, that build their own environment. The dams also turn streams into ponds and marshes that animals depend on.

It's Good to Go Out of Style

Experts estimate there were 6 million beavers living in what's now known as Canada when the fur trade started. At the peak of the fur trade, about 200,000 pelts were being shipped to Europe every year. By the mid-1800s, when fashions changed, the beaver was almost extinct. Slowly the numbers have increased as Canadians have realized how important this animal is.

WOULD YOU BELIEVE . . . ?
The world's biggest beaver dam can be seen from space! It is in Wood Buffalo National Park in Alberta and it's about 850 metres long!

READ ON, CANADA
Canada on the page

FINDING THE PLACE YOU LIVE IN THE PAGES OF A BOOK CAN BE A THRILL. CANADIAN WRITERS REFLECT THE NATION IN SO MANY DIFFERENT WAYS.

Anne with an E

It's hard to believe that a red-haired girl can change Canada — and the world. Especially if that young girl never existed! When writer Lucy Maud Montgomery created her world-famous character Anne of Green Gables, with her long red braids, she introduced her province of Prince Edward Island to many faraway readers.

Anne of Green Gables was written more than 100 years ago, but it is still finding new readers today. The book has been published in more than 20 languages and has sold tens of millions of copies.

The Hockey Classic

Did you know that *Anne of Green Gables* wasn't originally written for children? Neither was *The Hockey Sweater*, another popular kids' book. This story by Roch Carrier was first intended for adult readers. But a few years after it was made into an award-winning short film by the National Film Board of Canada, the story was also published as a picture book.

The Hockey Sweater told people about life in Quebec. This book was taken to the International Space Station in 2009 by Canadian astronaut Robert Thirsk. Here on Earth, the first lines of the story appeared for many years in both English and French on the back of the Canadian five-dollar bill.

WOULD YOU BELIEVE . . . ?

Alligator Pie, Franklin in the Dark, Jacob Two-Two Meets the Hooded Fang, The Incredible Journey, The Paper Bag Princess — these are just a few of the many incredible Canadian books that are popular with kids around the world. What's your favourite book by a Canadian author?

EVERYTHING ABOUT THE IMAX MOVIE SYSTEM IS GIGANTIC. GRAB SOME POPCORN AND READ ALL ABOUT THIS CANADIAN INVENTION!

Maximum Everything!

In IMAX, the largest screen is 30 metres high, about as tall as an eight-storey building. The film is so large and heavy that it needs a big projector: an IMAX projector weighs about as much as a small car!

The name IMAX comes from the words *Image MAXimum*. Founded by Canadians Graeme Ferguson, Robert Kerr, Roman Kroitor and William Shaw, the Ontario-based company is the world's most successful large-screen cinema system.

The Experience

In addition to the huge rectangular screens, there are dome-shaped IMAX screens that wrap an entire theatre. Called OMNIMAX or IMAX Dome, they're big enough to completely fill your field of vision, which makes you feel immersed in the film. It can even make you feel as if you're moving. IMAX films can take you down to the bottom of the ocean to discover the wreck of *Titanic* or out to space on the Space Shuttle. You can explore Earth's environment, go to a concert or ride a roller coaster in 3-D.

Although IMAX started in Canada, today there are more than 738 theatres in 53 countries. The company has won many awards for the ways it has changed movie making.

WOULD YOU BELIEVE . . . ?

Canadians have contributed to movies in many other ways. Until 1917, films were all black and white. Herbert Kalmus in Kingston, Ontario, came up with the idea of colour movies. The world's first documentary film, *Nanook of the North*, was filmed at Hudson Bay from 1920 to 1921. And before 1970, animated cartoons were created by artists making all drawings by hand. Nestor Burtnyk from Dauphin, Manitoba, computerized the process, making it much faster.

THE NORTHWEST PASSAGE
The top of the world

FOR HUNDREDS OF YEARS, THE NORTHWEST PASSAGE, A WATER ROUTE ALONG CANADA'S NORTHERN COAST, SEEMED LIKE AN IMPOSSIBLE DREAM.

The Fabled Passage

Early European explorers thought North America was just a slim island near Japan and China. When they realized how wide Canada really is, they then tried to sail over the top to reach Asia. That's when the search for the Northwest Passage began.

Ships and their crews perished attempting to discover it. The first time a ship finally made it completely through the route, it took from 1903 to 1906, with the boat making progress in the short summers, then being frozen in the ice during the long winters. It wasn't until 1944 that a ship made it through the passage in just one year.

The Passage Everyone Still Wants

Today, the Northwest Passage is back in the news because of how quickly its ice is melting. Some scientists think that summer ice in the route will disappear completely as soon as 2031. Shipping companies are keeping a close watch on the Northwest Passage, because if they can send their ships through, it could shorten their shipping routes by as much as two weeks, saving the companies a lot of time and money.

WOULD YOU BELIEVE . . . ?

A reduction in ice in the Northwest Passage will allow animals to migrate across the Arctic Ocean. For instance, a type of grey whale seen only in the Pacific Ocean since the 1700s has been spotted recently in the Atlantic. Scientists don't yet know how this will affect the oceans and environment.

ELIJAH HARPER
The Canadian who said no

ELIJAH HARPER BECAME KNOWN ACROSS THE COUNTRY WHEN HE STOOD UP TO CANADA'S FEDERAL GOVERNMENT AND DEMANDED THAT FIRST NATIONS PEOPLES' CONTRIBUTIONS, RIGHTS AND NEEDS BE RECOGNIZED.

A Quiet Strength

Harper was born on the Red Sucker Lake First Nation, north of Winnipeg. In 1981, he became the first Aboriginal person to serve as a Member of the Legislative Assembly (MLA) in Manitoba. In 1990, prime minister Brian Mulroney wanted the provincial governments to accept changes to Canada's constitution — the set of rules and laws that apply to all Canadians. The list of changes was created during meetings at a house on the shore of Meech Lake, Quebec.

All provincial parliaments and legislatures had to support the Meech Lake Accord for the changes to become law. In Manitoba, that meant every one of the MLAs had to agree to it. Harper was unhappy that First Nations people had not been consulted or recognized. Eight times the MLAs were asked to accept, and each time Harper quietly but steadfastly said no. The accord did not become law.

> "We want to be part of the Canadian society and to contribute toward the development of this country."
> — Elijah Harper

Back to the Land

Many people, including the prime minister, were furious, but Harper remained soft-spoken yet defiant. His determination united First Nations people and changed their lives. Harper became a celebrity; however, he didn't take his stand to become famous. "I am looking forward to getting back to the trapline," he said, "and looking at the stars at night."

Harper kept an eagle feather, a symbol of honour and strength, in his hand throughout the Meech Lake debates.

Canada's a big country, so no wonder its buildings and other structures are big, too. You'll find some of the world's longest bridges, tallest structures, longest canals and more here. Canadian constructions have to be strong, too. They must withstand blistering heat, freezing cold, hurricane-force winds and more. Find out about some of Canada's biggest building projects and how they link Canadians.

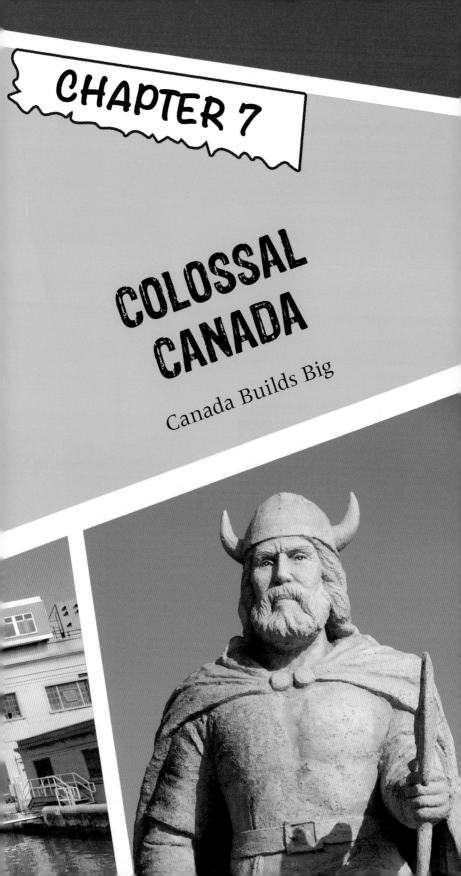

CHAPTER 7

COLOSSAL CANADA

Canada Builds Big

THE WORLD'S TALLEST TOTEM POLE
Head to Alert Bay

TOWERING 56.4 METRES TALL (HIGHER THAN A 17-STOREY BUILDING!), THE WORLD'S TALLEST TOTEM POLE IS AT ALERT BAY ON CORMORANT ISLAND, BRITISH COLUMBIA.

What Does It Tell?

The word *totem* comes from an Algonquin First Nations' word that means "his kinship group" or "family." Totem poles tell about a family's or tribe's history, membership and identity and also commemorate ancestors. Some poles describe popular legends or mark special events.

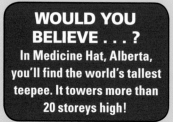

> **WOULD YOU BELIEVE . . . ?**
> In Medicine Hat, Alberta, you'll find the world's tallest teepee. It towers more than 20 storeys high!

Look Up, Up, Up!

Like most totem poles in British Columbia, the world's tallest totem pole was carved from red cedar tree trunks — three trunks, stacked on top of each other. It was carved by six artists from Kwakwaka'wakw First Nations tribes. At the top is a sun, with rays radiating out, and below that are a whale, wolf, thunderbird (a supernatural bird), bear and more. The animals represent families and tribes.

The pole is painted black, white, red, green and yellow. Black stands for power. White represents the sky and peace, while red is for war and blood. Green stands for hills and trees, and yellow represents the sun, as well as happiness.

> Toronto's CN Tower is Canada's tallest structure. In 1995 it was designated as one of the seven wonders of the modern world.

THE TRANS-CANADA HIGHWAY
Going for a l-o-o-o-n-g drive

IT STRETCHES FROM ST. JOHN'S, NEWFOUNDLAND, ALL THE WAY ACROSS THE COUNTRY TO VICTORIA, BRITISH COLUMBIA. AT 7,821 KILOMETRES LONG, THE TRANS-CANADA HIGHWAY IS THE LONGEST NATIONAL HIGHWAY IN THE WORLD.

From Coast to Coast

Canadians began asking for a highway that would join our nation back in 1910; however, construction didn't actually begin on the Trans-Canada Highway until 1950. It took until 1971 to finally complete the roadway, and it cost $1 billion. The Trans-Canada passes through all ten provinces and links the country's major cities.

Passing Views

Drivers on the highway speed through a wide variety of landscapes. In the Rocky Mountains in British Columbia and Alberta, there are snowsheds that protect the highway from avalanches. You can also find special overpasses to help wildlife safely cross the roadway.

Across the Prairies, the Trans-Canada is flat and wide open. In northern Ontario it winds through thick forests. Then the highway zooms along the St. Lawrence River through Quebec and into the Maritimes. Car ferries link Newfoundland and Vancouver Island to the mainland highway.

WOULD YOU BELIEVE . . . ?

The Trans-Canada Highway is the longest electric-vehicle-ready highway in the world. Electric vehicle charging stations have been installed so electric cars can zoom the roadway's entire length.

THAT'S ONE BIG BRIDGE
Hartland's got it

THERE ARE MANY BRIDGES IN CANADA AND THE WORLD, BUT THE ONE IN HARTLAND, NEW BRUNSWICK, IS UNIQUE: IT'S THE WORLD'S LONGEST COVERED BRIDGE.

Building Bridges

This bridge spans the Saint John River and is 391 metres long. The bridge's opening didn't happen as planned. It was scheduled for completion on May 14, 1901, but the night before, a local doctor received an emergency call from the other side of the river. Workers placed planks on the bridge so the doctor could cross and quickly help out.

Take Cover!

The original Hartland Bridge wasn't covered. But heavy rainstorms and snowfalls in the area led to the roof being added in 1922. Now the bridge is both a national and provincial historic site and when the bridge turned 111 in 2012, it was commemorated with a Google doodle.

The Hartland Bridge is known as a "kissing bridge." Back when people travelled by horse and buggy, a young couple who were courting could stop on the bridge and exchange a kiss without anyone seeing. That's why when it was first suggested that the bridge should be covered, many people were against it. They believed covering the bridge would destroy the morals of the youth!

> Years ago, when people travelled by sled in winter, snow had to be hauled into the bridge and spread over the floor so the sleds could glide through.

GIANT ROADSIDE ATTRACTIONS
Perogies, fiddles and geese, oh my!

TOWNS AND CITIES ACROSS CANADA HAVE BUILT HUGE, SOMETIMES SILLY, STATUES ALONG THE ROADWAYS. THEY ALL TELL SOMETHING ABOUT THE PLACE WHERE THEY STAND.

The Bigger the Better

If you're an animal lover, you can visit the giant goose in Wawa, Ontario. This town takes its name from the Ojibwa word for wild goose, *wewe*. In the town of Glendon, Alberta, there's a huge perogy, a Polish dumpling, that stands more than 9 metres tall.

Towns and cities across Canada have built huge replicas of everything from chainsaws (in Lillooet, British Columbia) and dinosaurs (Drumheller, Alberta) to fiddles (Sydney, Nova Scotia) and weather vanes (Westlock, Alberta). They attract tourists, tell what's important to the town or describe its culture or background.

Lobsters, Mosquitoes and Vikings

Shediac, New Brunswick, calls itself the lobster capital of the world, so it's no surprise that there's a huge statue of a lobster at one of the town's entrances. The name of the town of Komarno, in Manitoba, means "mosquito infested" in Ukrainian, so this village features a giant — you guessed it — mosquito. And don't miss the colossal Viking in Gimli, Manitoba, a nod to the town's Icelandic heritage.

Where's that perogy? I'm starving.

WOULD YOU BELIEVE . . . ?

Ontario is home to some major coin. Sudbury has a 9-metre-high nickel, Echo Bay has a giant loonie and Campbellford has a huge toonie. Cha-ching!

THE WELLAND CANAL
A grand water staircase

TODAY, HUGE OCEAN LINERS SAIL FROM PORTS ON LAKE SUPERIOR, THROUGH THE GREAT LAKES, TO THE ST. LAWRENCE RIVER, CARRYING WHEAT, IRON, SALT, COAL AND MORE. BUT UNTIL 1829, THIS TRIP WAS ONLY A DREAM.

Bypassing the Falls

Lake Erie is 99 metres higher than Lake Ontario. Before the canal was built, how could ships move from one lake to the other? They couldn't. After all, they couldn't go over Niagara Falls. Instead, Canadians built the Welland Canal, the world's tallest water staircase.

Eight Is Great

The Welland Canal is made up of a series of eight locks. These are chambers in the canal that have a gate at each end. Each gate can be opened or closed to allow water to flow in or out. When a ship is moving from a lower lock to a higher one, it enters the first lock, then the gate is closed behind it. Next, water is allowed to flow into the lock, bringing the ship up on the rising water to the higher water level of the next lock.

The gate in front of the ship is then opened and the ship sails into the higher lock. The ship continues through all the locks until it reaches the highest one and can sail off. It takes about 11 hours to travel all eight locks.

WOULD YOU BELIEVE . . . ?

The Welland Canal is part of the St. Lawrence Seaway, the system of locks and canals that allows huge ships to sail through the Great Lakes all the way to the Atlantic Ocean. It extends far into the centre of Canada and is the longest inland waterway in the world.

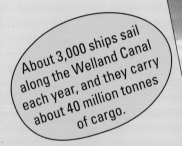

About 3,000 ships sail along the Welland Canal each year, and they carry about 40 million tonnes of cargo.

CONFEDERATION BRIDGE
An engineering feat

STRETCHING OVER THE NORTHUMBERLAND STRAIT BETWEEN PRINCE EDWARD ISLAND AND NEW BRUNSWICK, THE CONFEDERATION BRIDGE IS THE LONGEST BRIDGE IN CANADA.

An Icy Challenge

Confederation Bridge is also the world's longest bridge over water that freezes during the winter. The bridge is constructed from 44 spans, or sections, and each of those spans has supports, called piers, holding it up.

Those piers have to withstand thick ice in the Northumberland Strait that sometimes forms cliffs 10 metres high. So the base of each of the piers has a concrete ice shield. These shields act like the bow of a ship cutting its way through heavy ice. The shields force the ice to ride up and break apart. They can stand up to the force of 3,000 tonnes of ice — that's about 15 times the force that icebreaker ships in the Arctic have to withstand.

Talk About Big!

Right from the beginning, building the bridge was a big project. It was built using the world's largest floating crane, which stands more than 30 stories high. The crane moved posts and girders weighing up to 7,500 tonnes, yet could place them with great accuracy.

Since the bridge opened on May 31, 1997, potatoes and seafood can now move more quickly off P.E.I. That means exports of both have increased, which helps many farmers and fishermen.

WOULD YOU BELIEVE . . . ?
This area of the Maritimes is one of the windiest in Canada and suffers through ferocious snowstorms. Barriers along the sides of the Confederation Bridge shield the roadway — and prevent people who are afraid of heights from seeing the water so far below.

HYDROELECTRICITY
Harnessing the power

IT TAKES A LOT OF ENERGY TO POWER A HUGE COUNTRY LIKE CANADA. MUCH OF THAT ENERGY COMES FROM HYDROELECTRICITY, ELECTRICITY GENERATED BY THE ENERGY OF FLOWING OR FALLING WATER.

Renewable Energy

Unlike coal and gas, which provide energy but are burned and used up in the process, moving water is a renewable energy resource. Other types of renewable energy resources include sunlight, wind, tides and waves. As the Earth's population keeps growing, we will have to cut back on the power we use, or find new energy sources.

Fast-Flowing Water

Right now, hydroelectricity is fairly cheap to make, so it's the most widely used type of renewable energy in the world. Of all the world's countries, Canada produces the second-largest amount of this source of energy. Many of the hydroelectric stations, like the one above, are in Quebec.

Not only does Hydro-Québec produce enough power for the whole province of Quebec, it also makes enough hydroelectricity to sell it to other provinces and into the United States. The province has many fast-flowing rivers and waterfalls. The series of hydroelectric power stations built on La Grande River in the northwest part of the province is one of the largest hydroelectric systems in the world.

WOULD YOU BELIEVE . . . ?
Scientists looking for new sources of energy have been working on harnessing the power of . . . dirty diapers. The diapers are heated (don't think about the smell) so they break down into useful products such as fuel. One good thing about using dirty diapers: babies are always making more!

IMAGINE A STAIRCASE THAT'S 1,500 STEPS HIGH . . . AND MADE OF ICE. THAT'S WHAT CONFRONTED GOLD RUSH MINERS DESPERATE TO REACH THE KLONDIKE IN THE LATE 1800S.

Carrying a Heavy Load

Dreams of striking it rich brought droves of people to northwestern Canada after gold was discovered in the Yukon in 1896. But many arrived totally unprepared. The North West Mounted Police (NWMP) realized people would die unless they had enough food and supplies to live on while searching for gold, so they created a list of required equipment.

Are we there yet?

The full list — of food (including flour, salt, bacon and rolled oats), clothing, medicine and other goods — was strictly enforced and weighed about 2 tonnes. Miners arrived with all their supplies at the Chilkoot Pass, high in the mountains in northwestern British Columbia.

Don't Look Down

The Chilkoot Pass was too narrow for wagons or horses, so the miners had to carry everything in packs, making many trips. The trail was rough and walking was tough. In winter, workers cut out steps that became known as the "Golden Stairs." The stairway was only wide enough for one person at a time, so there was usually a long line of miners struggling up the steep, icy steps.

The Chilkoot Pass sounds like an extremely dangerous route, but it had been used by Tlingit First Nations for hundreds of years. It was the cheapest and shortest route for moving supplies to the gold fields.

WOULD YOU BELIEVE . . . ?

About 1,500 women journeyed through the Chilkoot Pass during the Klondike gold rush. They made the dangerous trek wearing long, heavy skirts, as well as petticoats and corsets.

QUEBEC CITY
A walled city

EUROPE HAS MANY WALLED CITIES BUT NORTH AMERICA HAS ONLY ONE, IN QUEBEC CITY. THE WALL WINDS FOR ABOUT 4.6 KILOMETRES AROUND THE OLD PARTS OF THE CITY.

Walls for Protection

The city was originally an Iroquoian First Nations settlement named Stadacona. But by the early 1600s, the village was abandoned — historians have no idea if the villagers were driven away by other tribes, killed by disease or suffered crop failures. On July 3, 1608, Samuel de Champlain, an explorer from France, founded the city of Quebec on the site.

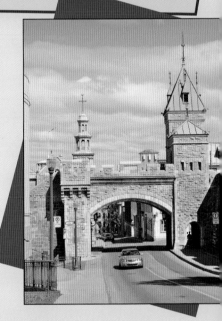

Building the Wall

Like most walled cities, Quebec City was surrounded by a wall to protect it. The first wall was completed in the late 1600s. As the British and French sides battled each other, the city came under siege many times. So a few years later, there was more wall construction.

The wall you can see in the city today was built between about 1745 and 1760. Hundreds of years ago, more than just a high stone wall protected the city. In those days, defending walls were made of earth, a ditch and, in Quebec's case, a *glacis*, which is a slight slope to hide the wall from the enemy. These all added up to a wall more than 75 metres wide.

WOULD YOU BELIEVE . . . ?

Quebec City's walls make it one of Canada's many World Heritage sites. These are sites chosen by the United Nations Educational, Scientific and Cultural Organization (UNESCO) because of their historic value and cultural appeal. Other Canadian World Heritage sites include the Nahanni National Park in the Northwest Territories, Alberta's Head-Smashed-In Buffalo Jump, and Old Town Lunenburg in Nova Scotia.

UNDERWATER OBSERVATION
Way deep down

ON THE OCEAN BOTTOM OFF THE COAST OF BRITISH COLUMBIA LIES AN OCEAN OBSERVATORY CALLED NEPTUNE (NORTH-EAST PACIFIC TIME-SERIES UNDERSEA NETWORKED EXPERIMENTS).

What's Going on Down There?

Since December 2009, scientists in labs and universities around the world have run deep-ocean experiments off Canada's coast. Thanks to fibre optic cables, the information the experiments generate is fed directly into NEPTUNE's website, where the scientists can access it.

Non-scientists, kids and anyone who's interested can also see and hear what's going on. NEPTUNE is the world's first underwater ocean observatory of this size that plugs directly into the Internet. It allows scientists to monitor ocean changes as they happen, as well as assess the effect that human activity is having on the ocean and understand how the sea floor, water and atmosphere are connected.

Let's Find Out!

Before NEPTUNE, scientists wanting information about specific parts of the ocean had to rely on ships that cruised by only infrequently or satellites that flashed by once in a while. But now, thanks to the world's first "Internet-operated deep sea crawler," scientists can send a data-gathering device to exactly the site that interests them, and soon have lots of information to analyze.

With more cables and new instruments, NEPTUNE continues to expand. It's been called one of humankind's "top ten most ambitious science projects."

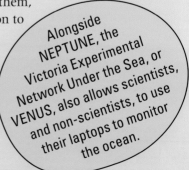

Alongside NEPTUNE, the Victoria Experimental Network Under the Sea, or VENUS, also allows scientists, and non-scientists, to use their laptops to monitor the ocean.

Do you love a good ghost story? Does the thought of a giant lake monster send shivers up your spine? Do wild horses fascinate you? Are you intrigued by tales of pirates and lost treasure? What about werewolves and curses? Canada has all that and more. Find out about ten spine-tingling Canadian tales.

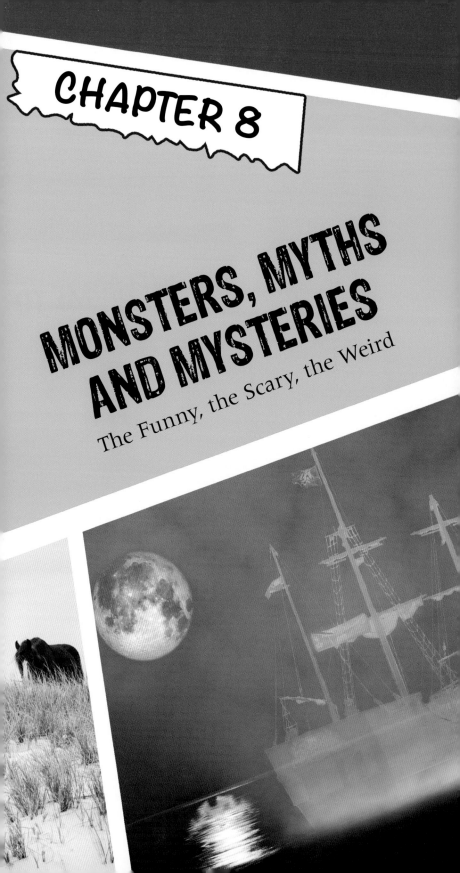

CHAPTER 8

MONSTERS, MYTHS AND MYSTERIES

The Funny, the Scary, the Weird

FIVE MYTHS ABOUT CANADA
Who made that up?

HERE ARE FIVE THINGS THAT PEOPLE AROUND THE WORLD SAY ABOUT CANADA, AND WHY THEY ARE (MOSTLY) UNTRUE.

#1: Canadians Live in Igloos

Igloos, traditional snow shelters built by Inuit, are a good use of snow and keep people cozy. But most of Canada doesn't have a climate where building an igloo makes sense, or is even possible.

#2: Canada Is Always Covered in Snow

Visit in the summer and you'll know how untrue this is. Victoria, B.C., has the mildest weather in Canada with an average of 2,183 hours of sunshine each year, flowers in bloom year-round and an eight-month frost-free season.

#3: The National Sport Is Hockey

It's true, hockey is BIG in Canada. You might even call it a national obsession. But hockey is only Canada's national winter sport. The official summer sport is lacrosse.

#4: Canadian Police Officers Dress in Red

The RCMP, or Mounties, do wear red but only on special ceremonial occasions. Most of the time they dress in regular police uniforms.

#5: Canada Is Just Like the U.S.

We share a language, cultural interests and a continent but there are many differences in geography, language, accents and words, food, government and more.

SABLE ISLAND
Is this place real?

A Home for Horses

Very few people live on the island but over 400 wild horses do. The horses, with their long, shaggy manes, are free and untamed. This magical place is called Sable Island. Since 2013, it's been designated a national park reserve.

WOULD YOU BELIEVE . . . ?
People have planted over 80,000 trees on Sable Island but because of all that sand, to date only one tree survives, a sturdy pine tree that's only about a metre tall.

How the Island Formed?

Scientists believe glaciers formed the island around 15,000 years ago, during the last ice age. As the glaciers pushed their way in, they gathered sand and gravel. When the ice melted, the sand and gravel remained. Today there's deep sand everywhere, which makes it hard and slow to walk.

How Did the Horses Get Here?

Most people believe that there have been horses on Sable Island since the 1700s. The British confiscated the horses when they expelled the Acadian people from Nova Scotia. The horses arrived on Sable Island via a Boston merchant ship. Sometimes the horses were used to rescue shipwrecked people and to help with livestock. But now the horses just roam free.

Around 350 vessels have crashed on Sable Island. The sand and the fog can be treacherous.

THE MYSTERIOUS DEATH OF TOM THOMSON
What really happened to Tom?

ON JULY 8, 1917, ARTIST TOM THOMSON WENT CANOEING IN HIS BELOVED ALGONQUIN PARK, BUT THIS TIME HE DIDN'T COME BACK.

Born to Paint

Thomson was born in Claremont, Ontario, in 1877. He worked in a machine shop but was fired because he was often late. He went to business college but dropped out. He began to paint and as soon as he did he knew that this was what he wanted to do with his life.

In 1907 he joined Grip Ltd., an artistic design studio. Soon he met other artists — many of whom would later become known as the Group of Seven.

Beautiful Algonquin

In 1912 Thomson visited Algonquin Park for the first time. The park became a major source of inspiration. If you've visited the park or seen a photo, it's easy to see that influence in a Thomson painting. In 1913 he began exhibiting his work with the Ontario Society of Artists. He was on his way! And then his life ended suddenly and mysteriously.

A Tragic End

There are many theories about Thomson's death. The official report noted that he drowned accidentally but some people questioned that. They believed that Thomson committed suicide after an unhappy romance or that he had been murdered. After studying all the evidence, researchers now conclude that Thomson did in fact drown accidentally.

WOULD YOU BELIEVE . . . ?
Shortly before his death Thomson wrote a friend that he'd be delighted if he could get $10 or $15 for a sketch. Today those same sketches can fetch up to $2 million!

THE LOUP-GAROU
Beware the werewolf

WEREWOLF STORIES HAVE BEEN POPULAR IN MANY COUNTRIES. FRENCH SETTLERS BROUGHT THEIRS WHEN THEY IMMIGRATED TO QUEBEC IN THE LATE SEVENTEENTH CENTURY.

Who Is the Loup-Garou?

The werewolves in sixteenth century French tales were evil sorcerers who took the form of wolves to eat children or devour a soul.

In the rugged landscape of Canada, the stories took on a new twist. In the Quebec tales, the loup-garou refuses to confess his sins and does not attend Communion at Easter. As punishment he's turned into a wolf every midnight. The only way to stop him is to stab him with a pick, preferably in the forehead.

The clergy told scary stories like these to warn people to follow religious rules and guidance.

Be a Good Werewolf

The good news for the loup-garou is that once he's stabbed, he's freed from his curse. The bad news for the person who stabbed him is that now *he* will become a loup-garou. But all is not lost! If the new loup-garou is pious and good and doesn't reveal his secret identity, he will turn back into a human in 101 days.

WOULD YOU BELIEVE . . . ?

There were so many reports and rumours of werewolves in eighteenth century Quebec that two wolves were killed when people tried to turn them into humans by stabbing them. Unfortunately for the poor wolves, neither turned into a human. They weren't werewolves after all.

MYSTERY AT OAK ISLAND
Sinkhole or treasure?

WHY IS TINY OAK ISLAND FAMOUS? BECAUSE FOR OVER 200 YEARS, THERE HAVE BEEN RUMOURS OF PIRATES AND BURIED TREASURE.

What's under There?

In 1795, 18-year-old Daniel McGinnis noticed lights coming from Oak Island, a small island in Mahone Bay, Nova Scotia. He investigated with friends. They found a depression in a clearing and began to dig. They discovered a layer of flagstone in the pit and pick markings on the wall. Then they found layers of logs. Something special had to be hidden there! The boys dug more than 9 metres but found nothing.

I thought you were bringing the shovels!

The Money Pit

The rumours and stories continued. Around 1803, a company started digging again. They found more flagstones, logs and markings but no treasure. The mysterious site was now called the Money Pit. And it was — people poured money into digging — but no money or treasure was found. Someone claimed to find a stone with symbols that stood for: "forty feet below, two million pounds lie buried."

Dying to Get Rich

Over the next century the pit flooded. In the mid-1860s, a pump boiler burst and a treasure hunter died. Excavations continued in 1866, 1893, 1909, 1935, 1936 and 1959. Over the years, six people have died in digging accidents. All that digging left lots of debris. It also inspired over 50 books, some TV shows, a video game and a display at the Maritime Museum of the Atlantic. As for the treasure: no one's found anything . . . yet.

> **WOULD YOU BELIEVE . . . ?**
> Franklin Delano Roosevelt, who became president of the United States, joined a dig in 1909 and kept up with news of Oak Island for the rest of his life.

THE MAD TRAPPER OF RAT RIVER
Silent, daring and dangerous

IT WAS RIGHT OUT OF THE MOVIES: AN AMBUSH, A CHASE, A WOUNDED POLICEMAN AND A DEAD CONSTABLE. AND FINALLY AN END TO THE STRANGE STORY OF THE MAD TRAPPER.

Who Was He?

The trapper called himself Albert Johnson. All anyone knew was that he arrived in Fort McPherson, Northwest Territories, in the early 1930s with a surly attitude, and lived alone in a cabin on Rat River.

Armed and Dangerous

Soon after he arrived, complaints were lodged that Johnson was tampering with animal traps. The police went to his cabin but Johnson refused to talk. When they returned with a search warrant, Johnson shot a constable. A more heavily armed posse laid siege to Johnson's cabin for three days. He fired at them. They fired back, but still he wouldn't come out. More Mounties arrived to surround the cabin but discovered Johnson wasn't there. The Mounties tracked him down and this time he killed a constable. That night Johnson scaled a treacherous, icy cliff in brutally cold weather and climbed high mountain passes. No one could believe his daring and resilience.

Tracked Down

Search parties, like the one above, were involved in the manhunt. Johnson had used caribou tracks and a blizzard to hide his tracks. He was finally discovered, cornered and killed on the icy Eagle River. He had $2,000 in his belongings.

WOULD YOU BELIEVE . . . ?

In 2007, Johnson's body was exhumed for a documentary and DNA tests were done to determine who this elusive outlaw really was. Despite all the effort, Johnson's identity is still not clear. And no one knows what brought him to the Northwest Territories or led to his desperate actions.

OGOPOGO
Is there really something there?

THERE HAVE BEEN MANY SIGHTINGS AND MUCH INVESTIGATION BUT NO ONE CAN SAY FOR SURE IF A GIANT SEA CREATURE LIVES IN LAKE OKANAGAN IN THE SOUTHERN INTERIOR OF BRITISH COLUMBIA.

What Is Ogopogo?

For years people have claimed they've seen a huge serpent-like creature, between 6 and 20 metres in length, in the lake. The creature is described as green, black, grey, brown or tan, with two or three humps. Some say that its head is like a snake's. Others compare it to an alligator, sheep or horse.

Aboriginal legends describe a lake monster or spirit that they call N'ha-a-itk (the lake demon). Aboriginal peoples paddled their canoes in the area with an offering of a small animal to appease the serpent. Lake Okanagan is deep, almost fjord-like — a good spot for a large creature.

Who Has Seen Ogopogo?

Since the late 1800s there have been many reported sightings of the creature. In 1926, there were several who claimed to have spotted Ogopogo. In 1978, while crossing the bridge from the west side of Lake Okanagan, Bill Steciuk was sure he saw the creature. Traffic behind him stopped and about 20 other people claimed they saw the serpent too.

Steciuk was so convinced he kept searching for Ogopogo. He did so in expeditions in 2000 and 2001. There have also been documentaries made of the Lake and Ogopogo, but no conclusive proof of a creature has surfaced yet.

WOULD YOU BELIEVE . . . ?

Some scientists suggest that Ogopogo might be a primitive form of a whale. Monster searchers are called cryptozoologists. Many say that Ogopogo is the best documented of all the lake monsters. It's been seen even more than the famous Loch Ness monster of Scotland.

MAGNETIC HILL
Yikes, it's pulling my car up

IT'S A SMALL HILL IN A RURAL COMMUNITY NEAR MONCTON, NEW BRUNSWICK. SINCE 1933, THIS LITTLE SPOT DUBBED "MAGNETIC HILL" HAS DRAWN TOURISTS . . . LIKE A MAGNET.

What's Going On?

For years locals noted that wagons rolled *up* the hill, which startled people and horses. After all, how could a hill make a wagon roll up? In 1933, editor John Bruce and reporters Stuart Trueman and Jack Bailey from Saint John's *Telegraph-Journal* decided to check out the rumours.

They spent hours waiting for the hill to pull their car up but nothing happened. Just as they were about to give up, their 1931 roadster rolled up the hill without them in it. Astounded, they wrote about the amazing event and a legend was born.

A Perfect Place to Start a Business

Soon after the article hit the newsstands, Muriel Lutes, who lived nearby, decided that given all the publicity it was a perfect time to start a business near the hill. She called it Magnetic Hill, borrowed money and opened an ice cream shop, a gift shop and a snack bar. Word spread, tourists came and Muriel's shops thrived. Soon more businesses opened. Today you can watch your car roll uphill (for a small fee) and also visit the water park, the zoo and a large concert site.

Why Do Cars Roll up Magnetic Hill?

Cars don't actually roll uphill. It's all an optical illusion caused by the slope of the hill.

WOULD YOU BELIEVE . . . ?
In 2010 a Japanese scientist won an award for duplicating the optical illusion that occurs on Magnetic Hill.

LA CHASSE-GALERIE
The flying canoe

WINTER, SNOW, THE FOREST, A CANOE, SOME LONELY LOGGERS, A TOUCH OF EVIL, A SPRINKLE OF MAGIC AND THE NEW YEAR ARE ALL PART OF A POPULAR QUEBEC LEGEND CALLED LA CHASSE-GALERIE.

How Did the Story Start?

When French settlers came to the New World in the seventeenth century they brought their stories, which often had a religious focus. One of these stories describes a wealthy nobleman punished for not attending church on Sunday.

In the New World, that story combined with a local Aboriginal tale about a flying canoe and it evolved into the popular Quebec legend of *La Chasse-galerie*. The most famous version, written by Honoré Beaugrand, was published in *The Century* magazine in 1892.

What's the Story?

In Beaugrand's version, a group of loggers are eager to return home to celebrate New Year's Eve with their loved ones. The devil suggests a deal. He will provide a flying canoe to transport the men home but on the way they must not touch a church cross and they musn't curse. They must also promise to return to the forest by six o'clock the next morning. If they disobey, they will lose their souls.

The loggers fly off. They have a wonderful time but soon they must return, so they hop back into the canoe. To their dismay, their navigator drives badly and they almost hit a church steeple. Worse than that, the driver swears, the canoe hits a tree and the men are all knocked out. Luckily, the story has a happy ending and they do not lose their souls to the devil.

At the opening ceremonies of the 2010 Vancouver Olympics a canoe with a fiddler flew through the air, celebrating the folktale.

GHOST SHIP OF THE NORTHUMBERLAND STRAIT
A burning ship

IMAGINE STANDING ON SHORE AND SEEING A BEAUTIFUL THREE-MASTED SCHOONER BURST INTO FLAME. FOR MORE THAN 200 YEARS, THAT'S EXACTLY WHAT PEOPLE SWEAR THEY SAW ON THE NORTHUMBERLAND STRAIT.

First Sighting

In the waters separating Prince Edward Island from Nova Scotia and New Brunswick, the first reported sighting of the burning ship goes back to 1786. Over the centuries, the sightings continued, often by groups of people standing on shore. One day the report of the flaming

phantom ship spread so quickly that the road was "black with cars as the curious came to see."

WOULD YOU BELIEVE . . . ?
There are reports of ships that have headed out to help the unfortunate schooner but as soon as they draw near, the schooner disappears into thin air.

What's Going On?

There are many theories about the burning schooner. Some believe that it's the ghost of two ships caught in a battle where both ships burned. Others contend it's an immigrant ship lost in a gale. And some say it's the *Isabella*, a cargo ship carrying lumber that disappeared in 1868.

Some scientists think it's an electrical phenomenon. Other believe it's a mirage, an optical illusion. And some think it's just thick fog reflecting moonlight. No one knows for sure.

There are so many reasons to be proud of Canada. Courageous and determined Canadians have improved the lives of millions, in our country and around the world. In such fields as exploration, peacekeeping and more, ordinary Canadians have achieved extraordinary results. Here are a few incredible Canadian accomplishments.

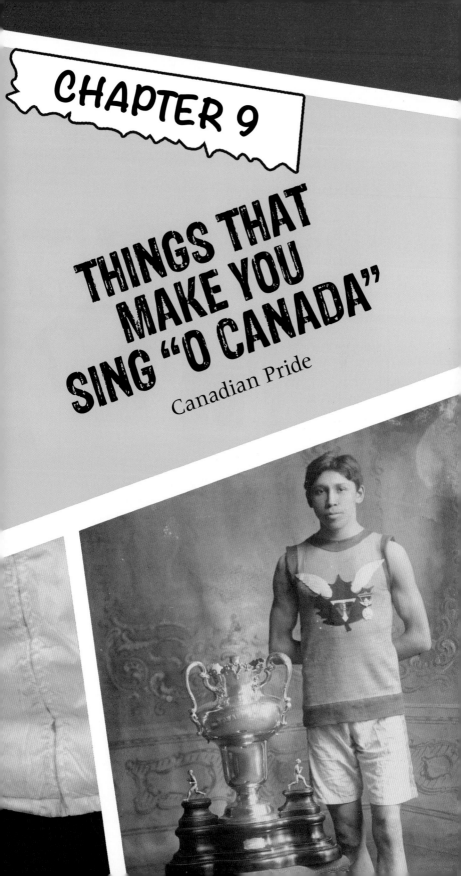

CHAPTER 9

THINGS THAT MAKE YOU SING "O CANADA"

Canadian Pride

HOCKEY GOLD
It's our game

ON FEBRUARY 20, 2014, HOCKEY-LOVING CANADIANS WERE GLUED TO THE OLYMPIC GOLD MEDAL WOMEN'S GAME BETWEEN CANADA AND THE UNITED STATES.

The Nation Watched

Yet again, Canada and the United States were meeting in the women's hockey final at the Olympics. Although the Canadian team had won the last three Olympic finals, it looked as if they would go down in defeat. The Americans were ahead 2–0, and the game was almost over.

But with less than four minutes left in the third period, Canada scored to cut the U.S. lead in half. Then, with the Canadian net empty, the Americans took a shot on goal — but hit the goalpost. The Canadians came back and tied the game with less than a minute remaining.

The Nation Cheered

Overtime was only a little more than eight minutes old when Canada scored again. The arena erupted — fans couldn't believe how the Canadian team had refused to give up. Three days later, no doubt inspired by the women's incredible play, the Canadian men's hockey team won gold, too. Canada's Paralympic ice sledge hockey team is also one of the top teams in the world and won bronze at the 2014 games.

WOULD YOU BELIEVE . . . ?
The first time Canada won hockey gold — at the 1924 Winter Olympics in Chamonix, France — the play was fast and fierce. One player was knocked out cold in the first 20 seconds, but went on to score two goals!

LONGBOAT'S LEGACY
Terrific Tom's run

ONE OF THE MOST INCREDIBLE MARATHONERS EVER, TOM LONGBOAT, BEGAN HIS CAREER IN A FARMER'S FIELD, WITH COWS FOR COMPETITION. HE WENT ON TO BECOME FAMOUS AROUND THE WORLD FOR HIS SPEED, ENERGY AND COURAGE.

The Making of a Runner

In the early 1900s, Longboat not only faced tough opponents on the track, he also battled racism. He was born on the Six Nations of the Grand River Reserve in southern Ontario. As a runner, he was often discriminated against because of his First Nations heritage. He also had his own ideas about how he should train and prepare for races, so he fought with his managers.

When Longboat raced, he seemed to put all these difficulties far behind him, winning marathon after marathon and often setting records. He was known for sprinting forward near the end of his races, with a spectacular burst of energy, while his competitors were barely still moving. This incredible runner was named Professional Champion of the World in 1909.

A Soldier's Calling

Longboat earned a lot of money racing, but he gave it all up to help his country by fighting in World War I. As a dispatch runner, he raced between groups of soldiers, carrying messages and orders. Longboat was often running through the fiercest battles and was wounded twice. Once, he was even declared dead! But Longboat kept running. When he wasn't speeding messages to officers and soldiers, he even competed in races.

> **WOULD YOU BELIEVE . . . ?**
> Longboat's nickname was "Bronze Mercury." He received this name because of his skin colour and because the Roman God Mercury is known for his speed.

IN FLANDERS FIELDS
The poem of war and remembrance

THE BEST-KNOWN WAR POEM EVER WRITTEN WAS ALMOST NEVER PUBLISHED. ITS AUTHOR DIDN'T THINK IT WAS VERY GOOD. LUCKILY, ONE OF HIS FRIENDS DISAGREED.

The Horrors of War

John McCrae, a doctor from Guelph, Ontario, had taken part in the South African (Boer) War. Still, he wasn't prepared for the horrors he experienced serving in World War I.

In the spring of 1915, McCrae was at Ypres, in the area of Belgium called Flanders. He worked without ceasing in his dugout medical station, even while dead and injured men rolled down onto him. When a close friend was killed, McCrae was devastated. He couldn't help his friend, but he could make sure these dead soldiers were not forgotten.

A Poppy to Remember

The next day, McCrae stared out over a nearby cemetery and the red poppies blowing in the wind, and wrote *In Flanders Fields*. But he decided it wasn't very good and he threw it away. Another officer found it and mailed the poem to magazines and newspapers in England. It was published in December 1915, and quickly became one of the most popular poems of the war.

Because of the poem, the poppy became the flower of remembrance for Canada, and other countries. People wear a poppy on Remembrance Day, November 11, the day in 1918 when World War I ended.

WOULD YOU BELIEVE . . . ?
Canada's greatest victory of World War I took place at Vimy Ridge, in northern France. Soldiers from other countries had tried to take over the ridge, but failed. The Canadians succeeded. They gained more ground and captured more prisoners than any other soldiers.

KEEPING PEACE
Pearson halts a crisis

JUST A FEW YEARS AFTER WORLD WAR II ENDED, THE WORLD WAS AGAIN ON THE BRINK OF A MAJOR WAR. THIS TIME THE HOT SPOT WAS THE SUEZ CANAL. IT TOOK A CANADIAN'S EFFORTS TO MAINTAIN PEACE.

A Hotly Contested Canal

In 1956, Egypt suddenly seized control of the Suez Canal. The canal is located in Egypt, but for years it had been operated by a company owned by the French and British. Egypt refused to let go of the Suez Canal, so France and England bombed the area. It looked as if the two sides would soon be going to war. The situation was very grim.

A Crisis Averted

That's when Canada's Lester B. Pearson stepped in. Representing the Canadian government, Pearson suggested to the United Nations (a group he'd helped create to encourage the world's countries to cooperate) that it form an emergency force to bring about a ceasefire between the two sides in the Suez Crisis.

Pearson's idea led to the formation of the United Nations Emergency Force (UNEF), the world's first international peacekeeping unit. His efforts worked. Canadians have been involved in every major United Nations peacekeeping mission since, in the Congo, Somalia, Sudan and many other countries.

In 1957, Pearson was awarded the Nobel Peace Prize, the world's top prize for peacekeepers. Pearson is the only Canadian to ever win it.

MEDICAL CARE FOR EVERYONE
A right, not a privilege

TOMMY DOUGLAS NEVER FORGOT THE FEELING OF BEING TOO POOR TO AFFORD MEDICAL CARE. HE SET OUT TO RIGHT THAT WRONG FOR OTHERS.

A Life-Changing Experience

The Douglases were facing a terrible problem in 1911. Their son, Tommy, had a bone disease in one leg. An operation could save the seven-year-old but the family couldn't afford it. It looked like Tommy was going to have to have his leg amputated. Then a doctor offered to operate free of charge. Tommy's leg was saved.

> "I felt that no boy should have to depend, either for his leg or his life, upon the ability of his parents to raise enough money to bring a first-class surgeon to his bedside."
> — Tommy Douglas

Realizing a Dream

When he grew up, Douglas became a politician so he could change the lives of poor people. He was elected a member of Canada's parliament in 1935, premier of his home province of Saskatchewan in 1944 and leader of Canada's New Democratic Party in 1961.

Douglas worked hard toward the goal that all Canadians should receive the medical care they required. He knew a national health-insurance program, or Medicare, could provide this. By 1972, all the provinces and territories had joined the program. Today it still makes Canadians proud to know everyone, rich and poor, can get medical care.

WOULD YOU BELIEVE . . . ?

Boxer, church minister, politician — Tommy Douglas was all of these. He's often known as the "Father of Medicare," and in 2004, Canadians also voted him the Greatest Canadian.

DINOSAUR PROVINCIAL PARK
Canada does dinosaurs

MORE THAN 500 DINOSAURS HAVE BEEN DISCOVERED AT DINOSAUR PROVINCIAL PARK, IN ALBERTA'S BADLANDS.

Digging for Dinos

Albertosaurus, Centrosaurus, Euoplocephalus — these dinosaurs and lots of others have all been found at Dinosaur Provincial Park. Nowhere else in the world have so many complete, or almost-complete, dinosaur skeletons been found in one place. There are at least 40 different species of dinosaur here.

Yay! A park!

Why So Many Bones?

When the glaciers retreated across the Prairies approximately 15,000 years ago, they gouged out vast areas of land. Luckily for dinosaur lovers, that exposed the ancient rocks and fossils below. Scientists think so many dinosaur fossils have been found here because the nearby rivers often flooded. Likely thousands of dinosaurs were drowned and quickly buried by flash floods.

Keep on Discovering!

Bones and fossils from Dinosaur Provincial Park can now be seen in museums around the world. And dinosaurs aren't the only fossils found here. The remains of flying reptiles, turtles and even crocodiles have all been dug up. Dinosaur fossils are still being found in the area, especially after heavy rainstorms when earth is washed away.

The Royal Tyrrell Museum of Palaeontology is named after scientist and explorer Joseph Tyrrell, who found the first dinosaur bones in the area, in 1884.

IMAGINE BEING TOLD YOU'RE NOT A PERSON. THAT'S WHAT A LAWYER TOLD EMILY MURPHY ON HER FIRST DAY AS A MAGISTRATE, IN 1916.

What?!

The lawyer said that according to the British North America (BNA) Act, which is the set of rules Canada was organized around, a woman was not a person. A year later, women's groups were pushing the prime minister to make Murphy a senator. Again, the answer was that because Murphy was a woman she wasn't a person.

Enough Is Enough

Murphy learned she needed a group of five to challenge the ruling. She gathered four friends who were already working hard for women's rights: Henrietta Muir Edwards, Louise McKinney, Nellie McClung and Irene Parlby. The group became known as the Famous Five. In 1927, they sent a petition to the Supreme Court of Canada — the top law court in our country. The court ruled that a woman wasn't a person. The Famous Five then took the Persons Case, as it became known, to the Privy Council of England, Canada's very highest court at the time. On October 18, 1929, the Council said the word "persons" in the BNA Act included women.

A plaque in the lobby of the Senate (shown above in 1938 with Judge Murphy's daughter at the far left, Nellie McClung at the far right, female senators and prime minister Mackenzie King) is a reminder that thanks to the Famous Five, women were finally legally persons and could hold any government position.

"The purpose of a woman's life is just the same as the purpose of a man's life: that she may make the best possible contribution to her generation."
— Louise McKinney

MAPLE SYRUP AND MUSTARD
Not necessarily together!

WHEN PEOPLE AROUND THE WORLD ARE ASKED TO NAME CANADA'S MOST FAMOUS FOOD, MOST SAY MAPLE SYRUP. MMMM!

The Sweet Stuff

For thousands of years, First Nations people in Ontario, Quebec and the Maritimes pierced the bark of maple trees in the spring to gather sap, the liquid that carries nutrients through the tree. The colourless, barely sweet sap was boiled until it was concentrated into caramel-coloured, richly sweet maple syrup. They taught European settlers the sweet secret of this delicious treat, and now maple syrup is loved all over the planet.

It takes about 40 litres of sap to make just 1 litre of maple syrup. Canada produces approximately three-quarters of the world's maple syrup. One of the best ways to enjoy this treat is the way First Nations people did long ago — you pour a thin thread of hot maple syrup onto clean snow, let it cool a little, then eat!

The Other "M"

Maple syrup isn't the only well-known food grown and produced in Canada. Did you know that no country ships more mustard around the world than Canada? The Prairies have just the right conditions for growing this plant: three-quarters of Canada's mustard comes from Saskatchewan and the rest is from Alberta and Manitoba.

WOULD YOU BELIEVE . . . ?

Some people make syrup using the sap from birch trees. It takes more than twice as much birch sap as maple sap to make the same amount of syrup, and the final product is rich and spicy.

MACINNIS EXPLORES THE OCEANS
A not-so-ordinary Joe

HE WAS THE FIRST SCIENTIST TO DIVE UNDER THE NORTH POLE AND HAS SPENT MORE TIME IN THE ARCTIC OCEAN THAN ANY OTHER SCIENTIST. NO WONDER JOE MACINNIS IS ONE OF THE MOST FAMOUS UNDERSEA EXPLORERS.

Diving Deep

Growing up, Joe MacInnis, who now goes by Dr. Joe, wasn't very interested in school. But maps showing Canada's Arctic and its oceans fascinated him. He learned how to scuba dive when he was a teenager and it changed his life. His goal was to study and get into medical school, so he could learn about the human body and how it adapted to strange environments. Not only did Dr. Joe become a diver and a doctor, he also became a photographer. In the late 1960s, he and his dive teams made some of the deepest and longest dives ever. In 1974, he made the famous first dive under the North Pole (above).

Finding *Titanic*

A year later, Dr. Joe found a fragment of a British ship that sank in the Arctic in 1853. Known as *Breadalbane*, it's the northernmost known shipwreck in the world. In 1985, he was part of the team that discovered the wreck of *Titanic*, the ship that tragically sank in 1912.

The Future of the Oceans

Dr. Joe has been diving for more than 40 years and has seen the effects that global warming, overfishing and pollution have had on the world's oceans. He works hard to educate people about the importance of these waters.

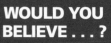

WOULD YOU BELIEVE . . . ?
Dr. Joe and his team of divers and photographers were the first in the world to shoot underwater movies of bowhead and beluga whales, as well as narwhals.

TWELVE-YEAR-OLD CRAIG KIELBURGER WASN'T LOOKING TO MAKE THE WORLD A BETTER PLACE BACK IN 1994. BUT MORE THAN TWENTY YEARS LATER, THAT'S JUST WHAT HE CONTINUES TO ACCOMPLISH.

Rights for Children Everywhere

Craig Kielburger was just looking for the comics in the newspaper. But when he saw a photo of a boy who'd battled bad working conditions and been murdered for his protests, he felt he had to do something. Along with his brother Marc and some friends, Kielburger founded a group that became known as Free the Children.

Since then, the group has helped improve kids' rights and build hundreds of schools around the world. The Kielburgers founded the organization Me to We in 2008 to create products produced in ways that respect the workers and the environment. This provides jobs, and the money raised helps fund the work of Free the Children.

More Young Canadians Making a Difference

When Alaina Podmorow found out in 2006 that girls in Afghanistan didn't have the same rights that she did, she started the group Little Women for Little Women. Alaina speaks out about women's freedoms and raises money for education in Afghanistan.

Ryan Hreljac is another Canadian kid who has improved the world. He was only in grade one when he began raising money to provide wells in the East African country of Uganda.

"Change starts with small actions that you can take every day. . . . nothing has the power to incite change like a group of passionate young voices, raised in unison."
— Craig Kielburger

WOULD YOU BELIEVE . . . ?

Kielburger grew up with a speech impediment so he knows what it's like to feel nervous about speaking in front of people. But now he gives talks to thousands of people in many different countries.

Canada is full of wonderful noises! Celebrations, parades and festivals bring people out to laugh, play music, sing and dance all year round. Canada also has many roaring natural wonders like Niagara Falls and icebergs — and even singing ones, too. Read on to celebrate each of these loud and wonderful places and events.

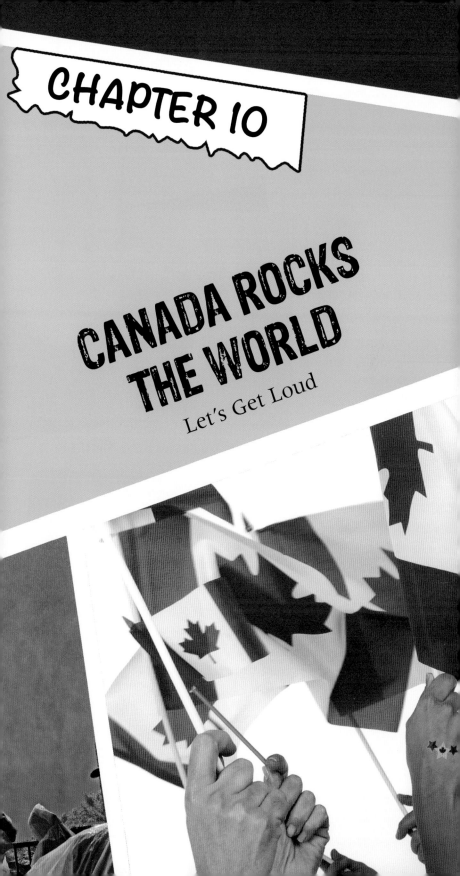

CHAPTER 10

CANADA ROCKS THE WORLD

Let's Get Loud

SINGING SANDS
La, la, la

SAND CAN BE HOT.
IT CAN BE SQUISHY.
BUT CAN IT SING?
IN FACT, SOME SAND CAN EMIT A SOUND THAT
MANY DESCRIBE AS SINGING.

A Sandy Sing-Along

A few beaches around the world have this unusual quality. One of the loveliest is on Prince Edward Island. Basin Head Provincial Park is also known as Singing Sands park. If you visit in the summer, you can drag your bare feet through the soft white sand and make it sing. You might even decide to sing along.

WHAT MAKES SAND SING?

There are three conditions that need to be met:

1. The sand grains must be rounded, shaped like a sphere.

2. The sand has to contain silica (silicon dioxide, a hard mineral that looks like glass).

3. There needs to be the right level of humidity in the sand.

Does Sand Sing around the World?

California's Kelso Dunes and Eureka Dunes, Warren Dunes in southwestern Michigan, Sand Mountain in Nevada, Porth Oer near Aberdaron in Wales and Singing Beach in Manchester-by-the-Sea (to name a few places) all have singing sands.

Despite its name and fame, not everyone calls the Basin Head sand sound "singing." Some say it sounds more like high-pitched squeaking.

ICEBERG ALLEY
Fizz . . . POP! Hummm.

ICEBERG ALLEY IS AN AREA OF OCEAN STRETCHING FROM THE COAST OF LABRADOR TO THE NORTHEAST COAST OF NEWFOUNDLAND. HERE YOU CAN SEE, AND HEAR, MAGNIFICENT 10,000-YEAR-OLD ICEBERGS DRIFT ON BY.

The Sound of a Berg

Icebergs are often born with a big splash and loud cracks of noise as these large islands of ice break off from a glacier. And they don't die quietly either. When an iceberg breaks apart, it's called an icequake. Underwater recordings pick up tremors, groans, pops and cracks that have been found to be as loud as the noise from 200 supertankers. When a piece of iceberg melts it makes a fizzy sound. The sound comes from the popping of compressed air bubbles inside the iceberg.

Where Do Icebergs Come From?

Icebergs are made of fresh glacial ice, not salt water. Most of the Newfoundland and Labrador icebergs start in western Greenland. It takes two to three years for the icebergs to reach Iceberg Alley. As they drift into warmer water, icebergs melt. Iceberg Alley is full of floating icebergs in the spring and early summer.

WOULD YOU BELIEVE . . . ?

German scientists have discovered that as an iceberg begins to melt it also makes singing sounds. These sounds are inaudible to the human ear but can be heard through special sensors. The sounds are described as similar to the hum of a beehive and the shrill sound of a violin.

SNOWMOBILES
Zooming on snow

SNOWMOBILES MAY NOT BE THE QUIETEST WAY TO GET AROUND, BUT IT'S EASY TO SEE WHY THEY WERE INVENTED BY A CANADIAN. THEY MAKE A LOT OF SENSE IN THE SNOWIEST STRETCHES OF CANADA.

Who Came Up with the Snowmobile?

Many people contributed to the invention of the snowmobile but one of the most important was Joseph-Armand Bombardier, a mechanic from Quebec who developed a propeller-driven sled in 1922. Bombardier also added the sprocket wheel and double endless track to make his snow vehicle even more practical.

When Bombardier's son died one winter because he couldn't get to a hospital in time, Bombardier was determined to make a vehicle to help in emergencies. He invented a seven-passenger snow vehicle. In 1937, he sold 50 of them as buses and for medical transport. Bombardier kept improving on his design. By the mid-1950s, his air-cooled, two-stroke engine Ski-Doo was introduced. It's the basis of most of the snowmobiles in use today.

Getting through Snow

If you lived in the Arctic or anywhere where there's lots of snow for a good part of the year, you might have trouble getting around without this way of skimming over the snow. Snowmobiles opened up winter life for many parts of Canada, allowing safer and faster travel — and fun, too!

WOULD YOU BELIEVE . . . ?
Snowmobiles and Ski-Doos can be noisy. Governments have restricted their use to certain areas and trails.

THROAT SINGING AND DRUM DANCING
The sounds of the North

INUIT WOMEN HAVE BEEN PERFORMING A KIND OF GUTTURAL SINGING GAME CALLED THROAT SINGING (OR KATAJJAQ) FOR GENERATIONS, AND INUIT MEN HAVE PERFORMED DRUM DANCING.

From the Throat

Inuit throat singing started as a way to soothe babies, or as entertainment while the men were away hunting. Two women faced each other in a standing position holding each other's arms. One singer began and set a rhythmic pattern. She stopped, left a gap and the other singer filled in with a different rhythmic pattern. The first woman to run out of breath or who couldn't maintain the pace lost the singing game.

WOULD YOU BELIEVE . . . ?

Christian priests once banned throat singing, but there has been a recent revival. Some of that renewed interest is credited to singer Tanya Tagaq, who combines traditional throat singing with pop music.

The Beat of the Hunt

Inuit men composed drum songs and dances while they were away hunting. When they returned home they taught their compositions to their wives. Many of the songs were about hunting in the Arctic. Traditionally the drums (called *qilaut*) were made of caribou skin. After the Europeans arrived in the 1500s, the Inuit began using the wood and nails from shipwrecks stranded in the ice in the frames of their drums. Drum dancing and throat singing are still part of many celebrations and ceremonies.

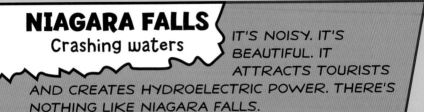

NIAGARA FALLS
Crashing waters

IT'S NOISY. IT'S BEAUTIFUL. IT ATTRACTS TOURISTS AND CREATES HYDROELECTRIC POWER. THERE'S NOTHING LIKE NIAGARA FALLS.

First Tourists

Explorer Samuel de Champlain described the marvel of the falls in his journal in the early 1600s. By the eighteenth century the falls were already a popular tourist destination. Tourism really got going after World War I with the popularity of the automobile, and it hasn't slowed down since.

Ours Are Biggest

The three magnificent falls that make up Niagara Falls lie on the border between Canada and the United States. The largest, Horseshoe Falls, is in Ontario. The two smaller falls, the American Falls and the Bridal Veil Falls, are in New York State.

Going, Going . . . Gone

About 12,000 years ago, after the last ice age, glaciers receded, creating the Great Lakes. On their way, they carved a path through the Niagara Escarpment and created the falls. Mighty as they are now, the falls are slowly and gradually eroding. Experts estimate that in 50,000 years, the falls will disappear. I guess we'll just have to take their word for it.

WOULD YOU BELIEVE . . . ?

Charles Blondin, a "funambulist" (a tightrope walker), crossed the falls many times in the mid-1800s. He even did it blindfolded.

IT'S BEEN HELD FOR MORE THAN 100 YEARS, AND CALGARY STILL DRAWS A HUGE CROWD EVERY JULY TO WHOOP IT UP, COWBOY STYLE, AT STAMPEDE.

Celebrating Cowboy Skills

Over a hundred years ago, Guy Weadick suggested holding a big, noisy, fun-filled show to draw the public to Calgary, Alberta, and pay tribute to the pioneers of the West. In September 1912, the first Calgary Stampede took off.

What Guy Started

Guy Weadick was an American cowboy and trick roper who performed in Wild West shows. While doing a show in Calgary, he found four financial backers to help him put together an event called the Frontier Days and Cowboy Championship Contest. Held in 1912, it ran for five days and drew 80,000 people to its parade, an astonishing number since Calgary's population at the time was a little over 60,000. It grew and changed year by year, and today the tradition continues with a ten-day party in July that still celebrates the skills of the cowboys who shaped Canada's West.

In 1912, most of the first prizes were $1,000, a saddle and a gold belt.

CANADIAN HUMOUR
Laugh out loud

CANADIANS ARE SO GOOD AT BEING FUNNY THEY HOST THE LARGEST INTERNATIONAL COMEDY FESTIVAL IN THE WORLD. THE JUST FOR LAUGHS FESTIVAL TAKES PLACE EVERY JULY IN MONTREAL, QUEBEC.

Get Yer Laughs Here

Gilbert Rozon started the Just for Laughs festival in 1983 as a two-day francophone event. In two years it expanded to include English humour and went on for a month. This laugh fest included acrobats, pantomimes and street performers. It's become very popular, now drawing the best and funniest performers. Talent scouts show up looking for the next great comedy star.

What Do Canadians Think is Funny?

Canadian humour often centres on family life, political events, politicians and culture. Early Canadian television comedy began with comedians Wayne and Shuster, who appeared on TV until the 1980s. In 1975, Canadian Lorne Michaels started a TV show called *Saturday Night Live*, which is still alive and strong on late night TV 40 years later. John Candy, Martin Short, Andrea Martin and Jim Carrey are just a few famous Canadian comedians. In 2014 Mike Myers became the first Canadian comedian to get his face on a stamp.

WOULD YOU BELIEVE . . . ?

There's a small community in Quebec called Saint-Louis-du-Ha! Ha! It's also the only town in the world with two exclamation marks in its name!

JEERING, HOWLING, HONKING, CLICKING AND SQUEAKING: IT TURNS OUT CANADIAN ANIMALS HAVE A LOT TO SAY! LET'S LISTEN IN.

In the Air

Have you ever heard a drumming in a tree that wouldn't stop? Has a high-pitched shriek from a bush made you turn around and look? Have you been startled by honking overhead? If you have, you've been around some noisy Canadian birds. The drum of the pileated woodpecker against a tree is so loud it can be heard up to a kilometre away. The high-pitched jeer of a blue jay may be a warning of danger. A flock of Canada geese communicate through their loud honking.

On Land

But it's not just birds that make noise. The wolf's distinctive howl may also be a warning to other wolves, or just a friendly hello to its own pack. Scientists think that wolf howling keeps wolf packs together. The howl can be heard far away, even across forests or tundra.

Under Water

Whales are the noisiest creatures of all. Each pod has a distinctive sound. Killer whales, or orcas, are found in all three of Canada's oceans but are most often seen off the southern coast of British Columbia. They click to help locate their prey and whistle and pulse to communicate with their fellow orcas.

WOULD YOU BELIEVE . . . ?

Killer whales are part of the dolphin family. Despite being related, they sometimes prey on dolphins (and anything else they can sink their teeth into).

LET'S CELEBRATE!
It's time to party

OVER 200 FESTIVALS TAKE PLACE IN CANADA EACH YEAR, CELEBRATED WITH MUSIC, DANCE AND FOOD. WHAT BETTER WAY TO HAVE A PARTY?

The Potlatch and Powwow

For hundreds of years on the northwest coast of Canada, Aboriginal chiefs and other wealthy tribesmen held feasts and gave gifts at potlatch festivals. Potlatch festivals are still held today but not as frequently as powwows. Powwows often take place in the summer and showcase Aboriginal music, dance, clothing, food and crafts. Some are ceremonial; some highlight dance and music competitions, and all are lively and colourful.

All Year Round

In the spring, summer and fall, there are many ways to enjoy Canadian maple syrup, sunflowers, peaches, apples and lobsters, and Canadians do just that at festivals. As for winter, Canadians know how to revel in that icy season too, with the Quebec Winter Carnival and Ottawa's Winterlude.

Celebrating Multicultural Canada

People from around the world who have immigrated to Canada have also brought their celebrations. A day spent at Toronto's Caribbean Carnival, Winnipeg's Folklorama or Edmonton's Heritage Festival (to name just a few multicultural events) is a great way to learn about the many — and tasty — traditions of the people who live in Canada.

WOULD YOU BELIEVE . . . ?

Celebrate Canada is an eleven-day celebration that kicks off with National Aboriginal Day on June 21 and ends with Canada Day on July 1. In between, celebrate Saint-Jean-Baptiste Day on June 24 and Canadian Multiculturalism Day on June 27.

CANADA DAY
A national invitation

MAKE SURE JULY 1 IS ON YOUR BIRTHDAY CALENDAR. THE COUNTRY'S BIRTHDAY PARTY IS THE BIGGEST CELEBRATION OF ALL!

First Birthday

On July 1, 1867, Canada celebrated its first birthday. That day Canada became a federation joining the British North American colonies of Nova Scotia, New Brunswick and the Province of Canada (now Ontario and Quebec). Bells rang out and bonfires were lit. Military displays, musical entertainment and fireworks filled the streets and the sky. But it wasn't until May 15, 1879, that a holiday was officially declared on July 1 and called Dominion Day. In 1967, Canada had a 100th birthday bash. By this time people had started calling the July 1 celebrations Canada Day. In 1982 that name became official.

How Do Canadians Celebrate?

Like many birthday parties there are balloons, funny hats and a cake. There are also fireworks, songs, parades, carnivals, barbeques, free music and flags. Special citizenship ceremonies are held. Each community celebrates Canada Day in its own way but the focus of the country's celebrations is in Ottawa, Canada's capital. Ottawa hosts large concerts, art displays and air shows by the famous Canadian Snowbirds. And after reading this book, you know that every day is Canada Day!

With colossal thanks to our amazing editor, Anne Shone
— E.M. and F.W.

ACKNOWLEDGEMENTS

With many thanks to publisher Diane Kerner, designer Aldo Fierro and proofreader Erin Haggett for their excellent ideas, suggestions and design. Thanks to Dr. Joe MacInnis for reviewing text and providing a photograph. Special thanks always to our wonderful husbands, Bill and Paul!

Photos ©: Alamy Images/Michelle Gilders: 14; All Canada Photo/ArcticPhoto: 121; Canadian Post Corporation: 72; Canadian Aviation and Space Museum/ Musée de l'aviation et de l'espace du Canada/CSTMC/Image Bank Collection: 50 top, 50 bottom; Canadian Press Images: 106 (Adrian Wyld), 43 (Deborah Baic/The Globe and Mail), 41, 78 (Jonathan Hayward), 79 (Winnipeg Free Press/Wayne Glowacki), 42; Canadian Space Agency: 53 (Anik-E Communications Satellite, 2005, Reproduced with the permission of the Minister of Industry, 2014), 49 (NASA); CBC Still Photo Collection: 52; CP Images/ Moe Doiron: 115; Dr. Joe MacInnis/Bill Kurtsinger NGS: 114; Dreamstime: cover top centre (Aladin66), 11 top (Chris Brignell), cover centre, 4 top, 10 (Debra Law), 32, 39 bottom, 80, 86 (Eranda Ekanayake), 87 (Gvictoria), 9, 17 bottom (Lostafichuk), 83 (Modfos), 36 top (Nicola Zanichelli), 39 top (Norman Pogson), 73 (Richard Nelson), 84 (Rusty Elliott), 90 (Songquan Deng); Dvids/NASA: 44, 48; Getty Images: cover bottom (Harry How), 30 (Paul Nicklen); Glenbow Archives: 99 (na-1258-102), 15 top (na-1338-111), 112 (na-3043-1), 59 bottom (na-588-1), 123 (na-604-1a), 12 (na-660-2), 38 (na-789-79), 89 (na-876-1), 17 top (na-936-7), 16 bottom (pd-392-1-1c), 11 bottom (s-227-231); iStockphoto/Julia Marshall: 92, 95; Library and Archives Canada: 69, 70 top (C-001350), 64 (C-002006), 102 (C-010627), 35 top (C-011371), 105, 107 (C-014090), 55 (Canada Post Corporation (1995)), 40 centre (Department of the Secretary of State of Canada fonds, e002113738), 40 bottom (Department of the Secretary of State of Canada, e002113736), 40 top (Duncan Cameron/Duncan Cameron fonds, e002282645), 18 top, 19 (e010957264), 70 bottom (nlc012101), 35 bottom (Norman Denley Collection, PA-066576), 98 (PA-014532); McCord Museum, M966.12.3: 4 centre left, 16 top; Nova Scotia Archives and Records Management/NSA Photograph Collection: 37 top, 37 bottom, 36 bottom; Ocean Networks Canada/ CSSF-ROPOS/Neptune Canada: 91; Shutterstock, Inc.: 15 bottom (Alexander Rochau), 57, 60 bottom (BGSmith), 68, 77 (bikeriderlondon), 94 (blojfo), 74 (Bonita R. Cheshier), 60 top (canadastock), 22 bottom (Cindy Creighton), 119 (David P. Lewis), 18 bottom (de2marco), 100 (EdCorey), 21, 27, 96 (Elena Elisseeva), 117, 127 (GoodMood Photo), 88 (Helen Filatova), 116, 122 (Igor Sh), 54 top (infographicSource), 104, 113 top (intolt), cover top left (Ipatov), 101 (James Steidl), 63 (jiawangkun), 75 (Jody Ann), 47 bottom (jps), 22 top (Jukka Palm), 67 (Justek16), 58 bottom (K.L. Kohn), 24 top (Karamysh), 85 top (LesPalenik), 56, 61 (Lorraine Swanson), 6 centre, 25 (Makhnach_S), 59 top (marialt), 5 top, 111 (Marques), 71 (melis), 29 (Micha Klootwijk), 4 centre right, 5 centre, 8, 13 (michelaubryphoto), 33, 34 (Mike Loiselle), 125 (Monica Wieland), 108 (Nailia Schwarz), 65 (nalbank), 109 (Oleksandr Kalinichenko), 58 top (Peter Wey), 45, 54 bottom (Photobank gallery), 6 top left, 124 (photosync), 24 bottom (Pictureguy), 62 (Rainer Lesniewski), 6 bottom, 81, 85 bottom (RHImage), 118 (rusty426), cover top right, 4 bottom, 7, 26 (Scott E Read), 126 (Sergei Bachiakov), 113 bottom (Stephen Mcsweeny), 31 top (Steve Collender), 110 (Steve Design), 51 (SurangaSL), 93, 103 (Susan McKenzie), 47 top (Tony Brindley), 31 bottom (TristanBM), 5 bottom, 20, 23 (Trudy Wilkerson), 76 (Twin Design), 120 (Tyler Olson), 28 (V.J. Matthew), 66 (Vlad G), 97 (Zacarias Pereira da Mata); University of Toronto Archives/ Jack Marshall: 46; Wikipedia/Owen Lloyd: 82.